D0606662

DISCARD

How to Use This Book

Look for these special features in this book:

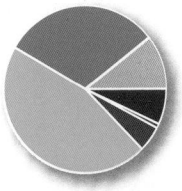

SIDEBARS, **CHARTS**, **GRAPHS**, and original **MAPS** expand your understanding of what's being discussed—and also make useful sources for classroom reports.

FAQs answer common **F**requently **A**sked **Q**uestions about people, places, and things.

WOW FACTORS offer "Who knew?" facts to keep you thinking.

TRAVEL GUIDE gives you tips on exploring the state—either in person or right from your chair!

PROJECT ROOM provides fun ideas for school assignments and incredible research projects. Plus, there's a guide to primary sources—what they are and how to cite them.

Please note: All statistics are as up-to-date as possible at the time of publication. Population data is taken from the 2010 census.

Consultants: Ellen Morris Bishop, Executive Director, Oregon Paleo Lands Institute; David Peterson del Mar, Author and Professor, Portland State University; William Loren Katz

Book production by The Design Lab

Library of Congress Cataloging-in-Publication Data
Kent, Deborah.
Oregon / by Deborah Kent. — Revised edition.
pages cm. — (America the beautiful. Third series)
Includes bibliographical references and index.
ISBN 978-0-531-28288-5 (library binding : alk. paper)
1. Oregon—Juvenile literature. I. Title.
F876.3.K36 2014
979.5—dc23 2013044361

No part of this publication may be reproduced in whole or in part, or stored in a retrieval system, or transmitted in any form or by any means, electronic, mechanical, photocopying, recording, or otherwise, without written permission of the publisher. For information regarding permission, write to Scholastic Inc., 557 Broadway, New York, NY 10012.

©2015, 2009 Scholastic Inc.
All rights reserved. Published in 2015 by Children's Press, an imprint of Scholastic Inc.
Printed in the United States of America 141
SCHOLASTIC, CHILDREN'S PRESS, and associated logos are trademarks and/or registered trademarks of Scholastic Inc.

1 2 3 4 5 6 7 8 9 10 R 24 23 22 21 20 19 18 17 16 15

BY DEBORAH KENT

Third Series, Revised Edition

Children's Press®
An Imprint of Scholastic Inc.
New York ★ Toronto ★ London ★ Auckland ★ Sydney
Mexico City ★ New Delhi ★ Hong Kong
Danbury, Connecticut

CONTENTS

1 LAND

From the Cascade Mountains to the Pacific coast to the high, dry Columbia Plateau, Oregon is a beautiful state with a diverse terrain. . . . **8**

2 FIRST PEOPLE

Oregon's first people arrived around 16,000 BCE. Their descendants developed bows and arrows to hunt for food and learned how to dry salmon. . . **22**

3 EXPLORATION AND SETTLEMENT

From 16th-century Spaniards to 19th-century Americans, people from all over the world explored Oregon. . . . **34**

6 PEOPLE

Oregon's friendly, down-to-earth citizens enjoy their state's natural beauty and heritage of many cultures. **74**

7 GOVERNMENT

Find out how the Oregon state government is organized and how it works to ensure the welfare of its citizens. **88**

8 ECONOMY

From farmers and fishers to lawyers, doctors, and businesspeople, Oregon calls on everyone to keep the economy strong. **98**

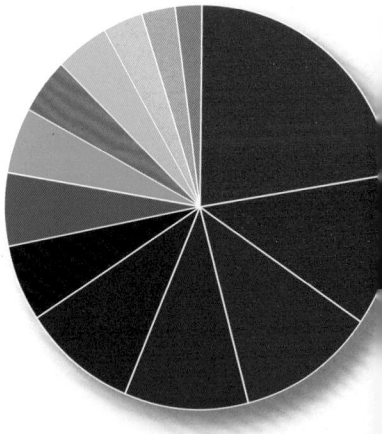

4 GROWTH AND CHANGE

The gold rush, farmers' quest for fertile land, and the slavery debate led Oregon to statehood. . . . **48**

5 MORE MODERN TIMES

Booming industries attract diverse peoples to work and live in Oregon. **62**

9 TRAVEL GUIDE

Visit Oregon's beaches, hike its trails, observe its wildlife, and walk in the footsteps of people who lived long ago. . . **106**

PROJECT ROOM

★

PROJECTS 116

TIMELINE 122

GLOSSARY 125

FAST FACTS 126

BIOGRAPHICAL DICTIONARY. . .133

RESOURCES 138

★

INDEX 139

AUTHOR'S TIPS AND SOURCE NOTES. 143

WASHINGTON
N
W
E
S
Lewis and Clark Campsite
Columbia River Maritime Museum
ASTORIA
World Forestry Center
Mount Hood Railroad
Columbia
PORTLAND
PACIFIC OCEAN
Tamastslikt Cultural Institute
Coast Range
Willamette
SALEM
Mission Mill Museum
Cascade Mountains
Deschutes
John Day Fossil Beds National Monument
John Day
Snake
Yaquina Head Lighthouse
OREGON
IDAHO
ONTARIO
EUGENE
BEND
National Historic Oregon Trail Interpretive Center
Museum of Natural and Cultural History
Newberry National Volcanic Monument
COOS BAY
Oregon Dunes National Recreation Area
Crater Lake
Oregon Shakespeare Festival
Great Basin
Rogue
MEDFORD
Klamath
KLAMATH FALLS
Oregon Caves National Monument
NEVADA
CALIFORNIA
0
50
Miles
QUICK FACTS
State capital: Salem
Largest city: Portland
Total area: 98,379 square miles (254,801 sq km)
Highest point: Mount Hood, 11,239 feet (3,426 m)
Lowest point: Sea level along the Pacific Ocean

MONTANA

Welcome to Oregon!

HOW DID OREGON GET ITS NAME?

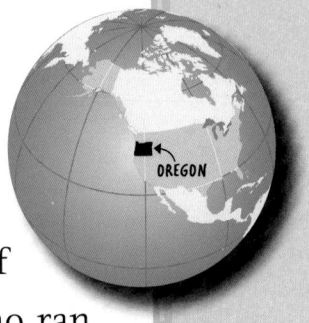

The origin of the name *Oregon* is a long-standing mystery. In the 1700s, a British army major learned from Native Americans near the Great Lakes about a mighty Ouragon River west of the Rocky Mountains. Early French traders who ran into fierce storms may have named the region after their word for "hurricane," *ouragan*. Spanish explorers may have called the land around the Columbia River's mouth "Aragon," after a province in Spain. It's fitting that a mix of people can claim credit for Oregon's name, given that it took all of them, and more, to make the state what it is today.

WYOMING

IDAH

COLORADO

UTAH

READ ABOUT

Getting to Know Oregon.....10

Molding the Land.....11

Land Regions 12

Plant Life 17

Animal Life 18

Caring for the Land.....21

A view of sunrise at Ecola State Park

LAND

★

IF YOU VISIT OREGON, YOU WILL OFTEN FIND YOURSELF LOOKING UP. Or down. Oregon's mountain peaks vanish among the clouds, and its gorges plunge into the distance. Mount Hood, the highest peak in the state, stands 11,239 feet (3,426 meters) above sea level. At Oregon's eastern border with Idaho, Hells Canyon marks the deepest gorge in North America—nearly 8,000 feet (2,400 m) deep! In southern Oregon, Crater Lake, at nearly 2,000 feet (610 m) deep, is the deepest lake in the United States.

Oregon Topography

Use the color-coded elevation chart to see on the map Oregon's high points (dark red to orange) and low points (green). Elevation is measured as the distance above or below sea level.

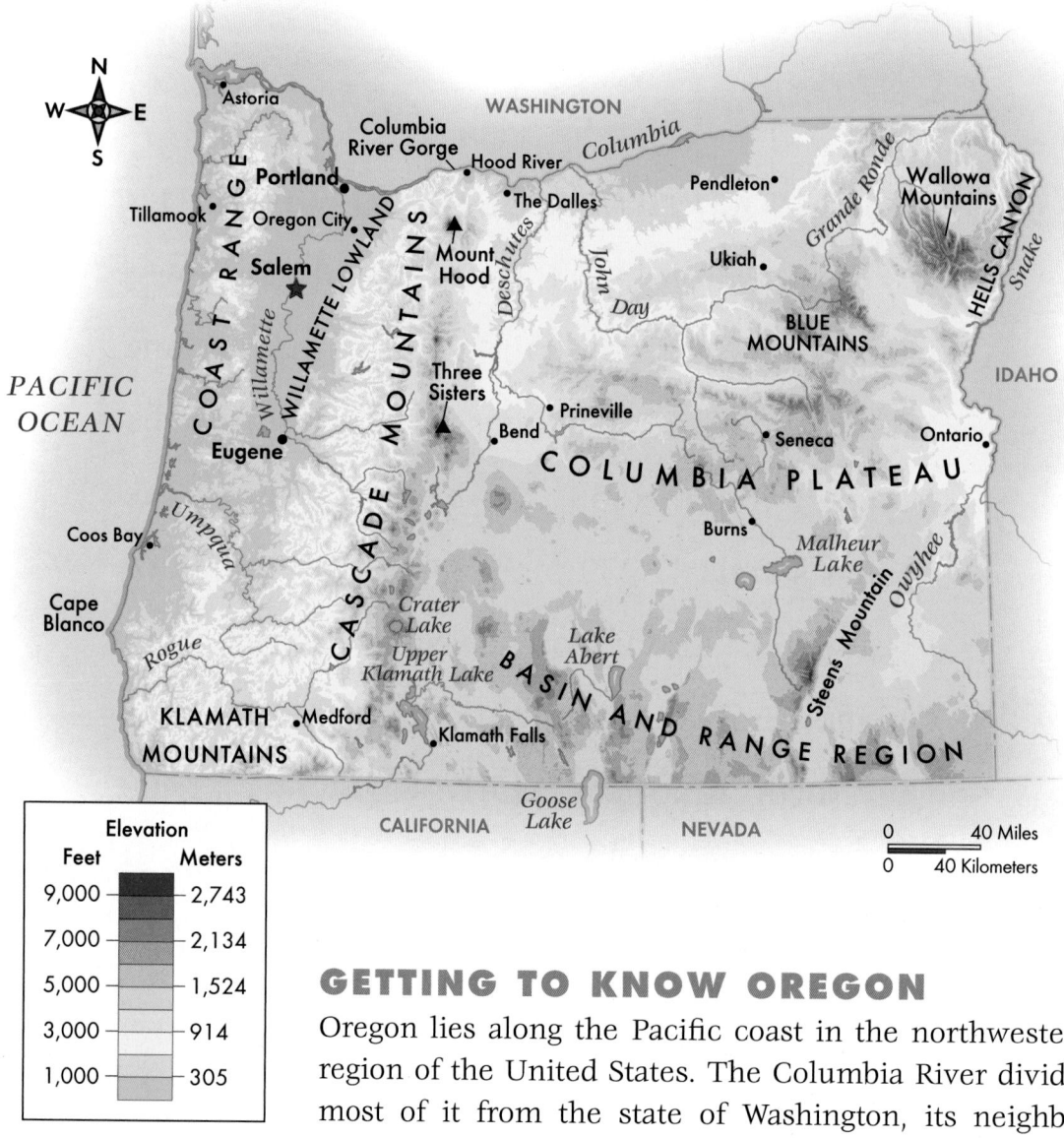

GETTING TO KNOW OREGON

Oregon lies along the Pacific coast in the northwestern region of the United States. The Columbia River divides most of it from the state of Washington, its neighbor to the north. Idaho lies to the east, and California and Nevada to the south. Oregon is roughly rectangular in

Oregon Geo-Facts

Along with the state's geographical highlights, this chart ranks Oregon's land, water, and total area compared to all other states.

Total area; rank . . . . . 98,379 square miles (254,801 sq km); 9th
Land; rank. . . . . 95,985 square miles (248,601 sq km); 10th
Water; rank . . . . . 2,394 square miles (6,200 sq km); 20h
Inland water; rank. . . . . 1,063 square miles (2,753 sq km); 21st
Geographic center . . . .Crook, 25 miles (40 km) south-southeast of Prineville
Latitude . . . . . .42° N to 46°15′ N
Longitude . . . . . 116°45′ W to 124°30′ W
Highest point. . . . . Mount Hood, 11,239 feet (3,426 m)
Lowest point . . . . . Sea level along the Pacific Ocean
Largest city . . . . . .Portland

Source: U.S. Census Bureau, 2010 census

When you add up all the islands, points, and inlets, Oregon has 1,410 miles (2,269 km) of shoreline!

shape. Its southern border is almost ruler-straight. The northern edge curves gently with the natural bends of the Columbia, and the Snake River forms part of the border with Idaho. The Pacific coast is jagged with bays, inlets, and rocky islands.

MOLDING THE LAND

The earth's crust is made up of giant plates that fit together roughly like the pieces of a jigsaw puzzle. Slowly and relentlessly, these plates move from place to place. More than 100 million years ago, Oregon's first land was formed. It lay on the western rim of the North American plate.

As this plate pushed westward, it collided with other plates and islands off its coast. The islands it nudged up

A couple canoes on Sparks Lake near Broken Top Mountain in the Cascade Range.

against had been formed by undersea volcanoes. These islands became mountains on the mainland as Oregon grew. As the North American plate, with its newly added Oregon land, continued to move westward, it pushed over the Pacific seafloor. Deep beneath the surface, rock began to melt. The melted rock rose toward the surface, creating volcanoes, including the Cascade Range. Some of these volcanoes are still active today.

LAND REGIONS

Oregon's mountains and valleys divide the state into several distinct areas. Some experts divide Oregon into seven land regions: the Coast Range Region, the Willamette Lowland, the Cascade Mountains, the Klamath Mountains, the Columbia **Plateau**, the Blue Mountains and Hells Canyon, and the Basin and Range Region.

WORD TO KNOW

plateau *an elevated part of the earth with steep slopes*

Coast Range Region

Along the Oregon coast, pounding waves have carved spectacular cliffs. Although parts of Oregon's coast are rocky and rugged, the state also has many beautiful beaches. In some places, the wind has gathered beach sand into great hills called dunes. Natural rock sculptures called sea stacks tower offshore.

Along Oregon's Pacific coast are a series of low, rolling mountain ranges. The Coast Ranges, as they are called, are the lowest mountains in the state. They average about 1,500 feet (457 m) in height. In many spots, sheer cliffs rise from the sea. In other places, the mountains are like a series of steps.

Willamette Lowland

Between the Coast Range Region and the Cascades lies the fertile Willamette Lowland. The Willamette River and its branches drain most of the lowland. The Willamette River is a major **tributary** of the Columbia, North America's fourth-largest river.

With its heavy flow and steep drop, the Columbia River generates more hydroelectric power than any river in North America.

WORDS TO KNOW

tributary *a river that flows into a larger river*

hydroelectric power *electricity generated by the force of water passing over a dam*

A photographer captures the scenery of Cape Kiwanda along the Oregon coast.

Cascade Mountains

The beautiful Cascade Mountains run like a spine down Oregon from north to south. The state's loftiest peaks rise in this range. Mount Hood towers 11,239 feet (3,426 m) above sea level. Hot springs gurgle near the summit of this active volcano. Mount Jefferson rises 10,495 feet (3,199 m). The Three Sisters are a cluster of peaks, each more than 10,000 feet (3,000 m) tall. The catastrophic eruption of an ancient volcano called Mount Mazama formed Crater Lake in the southern Cascades. The lake and the surrounding scenic area are preserved within Crater Lake National Park.

WOW

Crater Lake is the seventh-deepest lake in the world!

Klamath Mountains

More rugged peaks stand in the Klamath Mountains, which span southwestern Oregon and northwestern California. These mountains include some of Oregon's oldest rocks. Oregon's highest peak in this range is Mount Ashland, at 7,533 feet (2,296 m). In the north, the Klamaths are called the Siskiyou Mountains. Many parts of this region are preserved as wilderness areas.

Hikers along the edge of Crater Lake

The Snake River runs through Hells Canyon.

The Columbia Plateau

This high, dry rugged plateau spreads east of the Cascades. The John Day and Deschutes rivers, which form deep scenic gorges, cut through the plateau.

The Blue Mountains and Hells Canyon

Oregon's oldest rocks and deepest gorge are found in its northeastern corner. **Glaciers** carved the region's Wallowa and Elkhorn mountains, which reach almost 10,000 feet (3,000 m) high. Hells Canyon, which lies on the border between Oregon and Idaho, is the deepest river gorge in North America. From the rim on the Oregon side, you can see the Snake River flowing more than a mile below you. The canyon is 10 miles (16 km) wide at its broadest point.

The Basin and Range Region

Oregon's southeastern corner lies within the Basin and Range Region. This region extends south into Nevada. It is a dry area of steep-sided mountains and bowl-shaped valleys called basins. Steens Mountain rises high above the surrounding desert land.

WORD TO KNOW

glaciers *slow-moving masses of ice*

Weather Report

This chart shows record temperatures (high and low) for the state, as well as average temperatures (July and January) and average annual precipitation.

Record high temperature . . . . . 119°F (48°C)
at Prineville on July 29, 1898, and at Pendleton on August 10, 1898
Record low temperature . . . . . –54°F (–48°C)
at Ukiah on February 9, 1933, and at Seneca on February 10, 1933
Average July temperature, Portland . . . . . 68°F (20°C)
Average January temperature, Portland . . . . . 41°F (5°C)
Average annual precipitation, Portland . . . . . 36 inches (91 cm)

Source: National Climatic Data Center, NESDIS, NOAA, U.S. Department of Commerce

CLIMATE

When it comes to weather, Oregon is all over the map. That is to say, the state's climate differs widely from one region to another. Oregon has sun-parched expanses, snowcapped mountains, and even some of the cloudiest and rainiest spots in the country.

Warm, moist breezes from the Pacific fan the coast of Oregon. Places west of the Cascades tend to have a mild climate and receive generous rainfall. Some places on the west slopes of the Coast Ranges get up to 200 inches (508 centimeters) of rain each year.

The mighty Cascades form a barrier, blocking rain-laden winds from reaching the eastern part of the state. When you travel east over the mountains, you see a dramatic change. Within a few minutes, you pass from the green, forested western slopes to the open grasslands on the eastern side. While western Oregon is wet, especially in the winter, portions of the eastern two-thirds of the state may receive as little as 15 inches (38 cm) of rain a year. The driest parts of Oregon are in the Columbia Plateau and the Basin and Range.

WOW

Portland is one of the cloudiest cities in the United States. In an average year, the sun breaks through only 39 percent of the time during daylight hours!

ROUGH WEATHER!

Although the climate in Oregon is generally mild, fierce windstorms and unusually heavy rains sometimes pound the state. On Columbus Day, October 12, 1962, a windstorm battered the Oregon coast and caused major damage as far east as the Willamette Valley. It destroyed homes and barns and uprooted thousands of trees. Heavy rains in January and February 1996 caused many streams and rivers in western Oregon to overflow their banks, resulting in major flood damage in Oregon City and Tillamook. Ten years later, on December 14–15, 2006, a Pacific storm with high winds and heavy rain struck Oregon and Washington. Some 350,000 people in Oregon lost power, and eight people were reported dead or missing.

Oregon National Park Areas

This map shows some of Oregon's national parks, monuments, preserves, and other areas protected by the National Park Service.

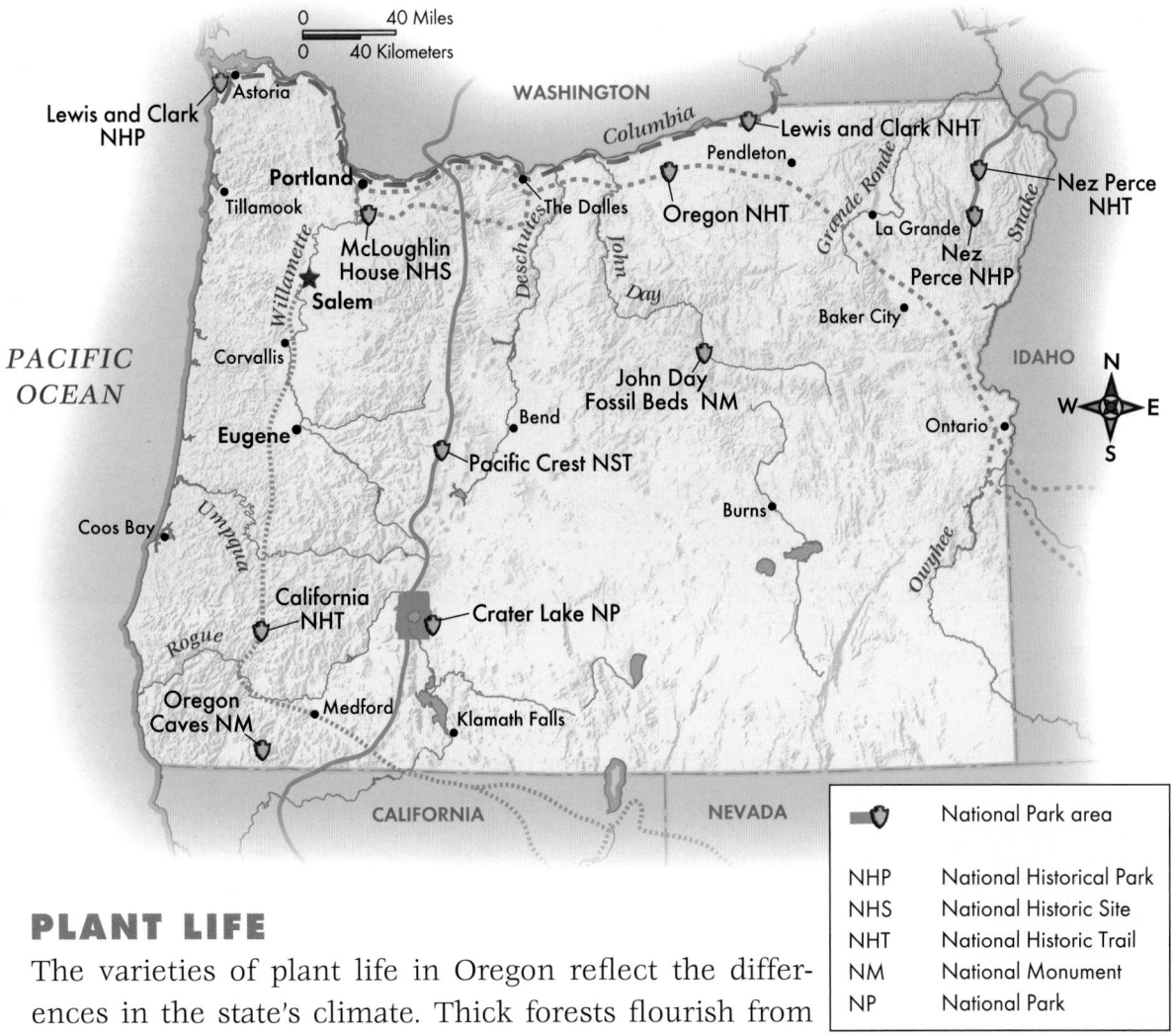

PLANT LIFE

The varieties of plant life in Oregon reflect the differences in the state's climate. Thick forests flourish from the coast to the western slopes of the Cascades. Pines and redwoods tower more than 100 feet (30 m) above the ground. Cedars, spruces, hemlocks, willows, and cottonwoods grow on hillsides and along streams. The dominant tree in western Oregon is the Douglas fir.

Many elk make their home in Oregon forests.

Several kinds of sagebrush grow in arid eastern Oregon. Though it is dry, this part of the state supports some tall trees, especially the stately ponderosa pine.

Many species of wildflowers bloom in Oregon. Among them are buttercups, Indian pipes, and Oregon grapes, Oregon's state flower.

Marmot

ANIMAL LIFE

Oregon's forests shelter many mammals, including foxes, coyotes, bobcats, and raccoons. The call of the marmot (a rodent similar to a woodchuck) is heard in the high Cascades. In the 1800s, hunting killed off several species in eastern Oregon that have since been reintroduced, including elk, mountain goats, and bighorn sheep.

ENDANGERED SPECIES

Oregon has several animal species listed as threatened or endangered, including the northern spotted owl, the Lahontan cutthroat trout, and several kinds of salmon. Many Oregon plant species are also listed as threatened or endangered, including the golden paintbrush, the Willamette daisy, Kincaid's lupine, and MacFarlane's four-o'clock.

Northern spotted owl

By the 1940s, gray wolves had been hunted to extinction in the state. Wolves that were not killed in Oregon relocated to Idaho. By 2006, small numbers of wolves began to reappear in Oregon. In 2012, restrictions on wolf hunting were established, and the wolf population increased from 29 to 46.

Black bears and cougars prowl the mountains. Mule deer, black-tailed deer, and elk graze in mountain meadows. Whales and porpoises cavort along the coast. Playful sea otters swim near the mouths of Oregon's coastal rivers.

Oregon's streams are home to many different fish, including perch, bass, and steelhead trout. Salmon spend most of their lives in the ocean but battle their way upstream to lay eggs.

In the spring, forests and grasslands ring with birdsong. The flute-voiced western meadowlark is Oregon's state bird. Other songbirds include the hermit thrush, the wood peewee, and the western bluebird. The bald eagle and the golden eagle are breathtaking sights as they circle in search of prey.

MINI-BIO

OPAL WHITELEY: A CHILD OF NATURE

As a child, Opal Whiteley (1897–1992) loved the birds and animals near her home in Walden. As a teenager, she began to teach classes about the natural world to children and adults around the state. A 1920 best seller called *The Story of Opal: The Journal of an Understanding Heart* claimed to be based on a diary Whiteley began at the age of six. With her deep love of nature, she became an important symbol for many who sought to preserve Oregon's natural beauty. Her life has inspired several books and even a Broadway musical titled *Opal*.

Want to know more? Visit www.factsfornow.scholastic.com and enter the keyword **Oregon**.

THINK ABOUT IT!

Saving Old-Growth Forests

During the late 1980s and early 1990s, the northern spotted owl, a little-known bird of the Northwest, became the subject of a fierce controversy. The northern spotted owl lives in old-growth forest—that is, forest that has never been cut for timber. A wide variety of trees and smaller plants grow in old-growth forest, which makes it a unique natural environment. The northern spotted owl is one of several species that require this environment in order to survive. Its presence is considered an indicator of the health and stability of the entire environment. In the early decades of the 20th century, vast tracts of Oregon's old-growth forest fell to the logger's ax. By 1990, only a small percentage of the state's original forest remained intact.

If the last old-growth forests were logged, the number of northern spotted owls would surely decrease. According to federal law, an industry cannot destroy the habitat of an endangered species. Environmentalists saw the plight of the northern spotted owl as a way to save the last old-growth forests in Oregon. They filed lawsuits to stop future logging in the owl's habitat.

Thousands of people in rural Oregon depend on logging for their livelihood. Loggers and their families were angry and frightened by efforts to halt the cutting of old-growth timber. Bumper stickers proclaimed, "I VOTE JOBS, NOT OWLS!" After some logging was stopped, residents complained about drops in wages and lost jobs.

As a result of the lawsuits, logging in the old-growth forests dropped sharply. Many loggers had to change jobs. But as Jerry Franklin, a scientist at the University of Washington, points out, "There is no hope for the spotted owl without habitat." Scientists continue to work to try to save the spotted owl and the magnificent forests in which it and many species live.

A salmon ladder at the Bonneville Dam on the Columbia River

CARING FOR THE LAND

Many laws in Oregon protect the state's air, water, and other resources. The state was at the forefront of the movement to require deposits on beverage containers as a way to encourage people to recycle them, which, in turn, helps cut down on roadside litter. Most of Oregon's beaches and coastal bluffs are preserved as public parkland. Salmon ladders help salmon swim over dams on their upstream journey to lay their eggs, and in some streams, dams are being removed to help fish and wildlife. Concerned Oregonians value the environment and want to preserve it for future generations.

READ ABOUT

People of the Columbia Plateau 26

People of the Basin and Range.... 27

People of the Coast 28

Hoofprints on the Grasslands ... 32

Prehistoric people used spears to hunt large game animals.

c. 16,000 BCE
People first enter what is now Oregon

2500 BCE ▲
People on the Columbia River learn to dry and store salmon

c. 1000 BCE
People learn to hunt with bows and arrows

CHAPTER TWO

FIRST PEOPLE

★

PEOPLE FIRST ENTERED NORTH AMERICA FROM ASIA WHEN GREAT GLACIERS CONNECTED THE TWO CONTINENTS. These hunters followed herds of mammoths and other large game animals. Gradually, the ice sheet melted, the sea level rose, and water separated Asia from North America. People first arrived in what is now Oregon in about 16,000 BCE.

500 CE

A trading center develops at the site of The Dalles

1720s ►

Horses reach the Columbia Plateau

1805

Nez Perces meet with the region's first white visitors

WOW

Archaeologists found a collection of sagebrush sandals in an Oregon cave that are thought to be 10,000 years old.

WORDS TO KNOW

archaeologists *people who study the remains of past human societies*

pemmican *dried meat that was sometimes mixed with dried berries*

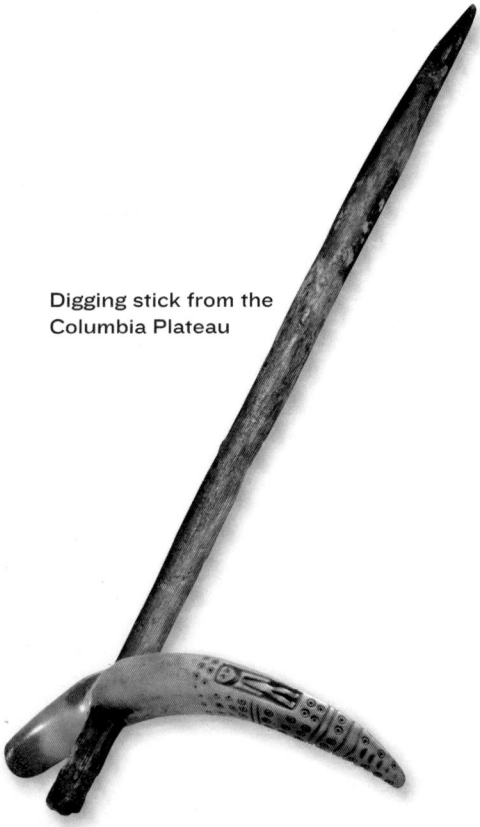

Digging stick from the Columbia Plateau

EARLY PEOPLES

Oregon's first people hunted with spears and fished with hooks made of bone. These people lived in small family groups, moving from place to place as they followed the herds. For the people along Oregon's rivers and streams, life revolved around the yearly migration of the salmon. As great schools of salmon headed upstream to lay their eggs, people waited along the banks with nets and spears. But food was plentiful only while the salmon run lasted. There was no way to preserve extra fish for any leaner times ahead.

Sometime around 2500 BCE, people near the present-day city of The Dalles discovered they could dry salmon on wooden racks in the sun. Carefully dried salmon, or **pemmican**, became a valuable food. Pemmican could be stored for months or even years at a time. It was rich in protein and vitamins. Eventually, this food was in great demand by people who lived farther inland. By around 500 CE, The Dalles became a lively trading center. People from all over the Northwest traveled there to trade for pemmican and other goods.

Forests were filled with deer, elk, and bears. In about 1000 BCE, hunters developed bows and arrows. These were good weapons to use when hunting small game, because the arrows could be fired with great accuracy.

Ways of life varied greatly among Oregon's early people. Along the coast and lower end of the Columbia River, people settled in villages. A powerful chief headed each village, and some families were wealthier than others. On the Columbia Plateau and in the Great Basin, people lived in small groups that were always on the move. In general, people within these bands had equal standing with one another. The hardships of day-to-day life kept anyone from gathering much wealth.

Native American Peoples

(Before European Contact)

This map shows the general area of Native American peoples before European settlers arrived.

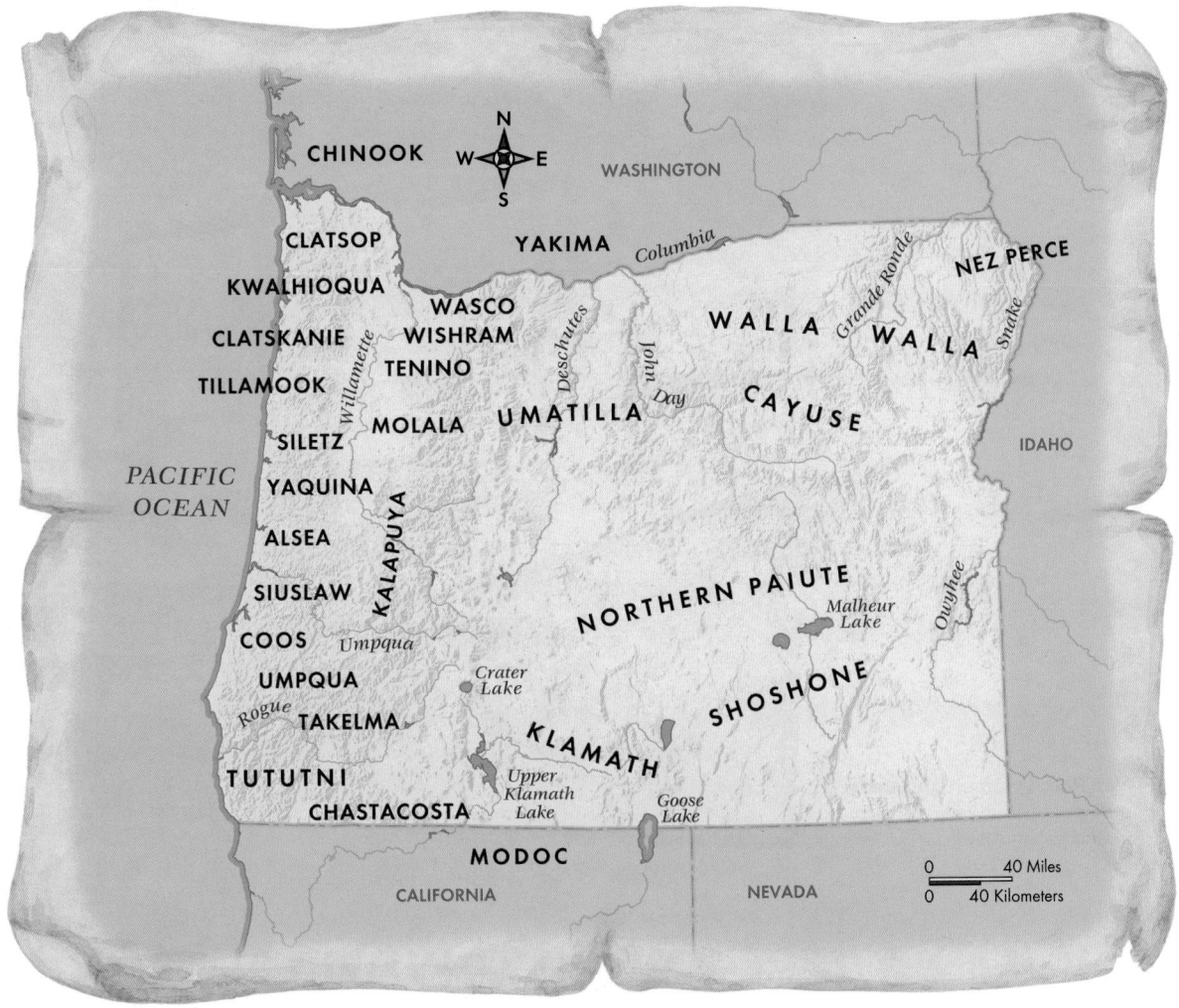

By the late 1700s, about two dozen languages were spoken in what is now Oregon. There may have been as many as 50 distinct groups. These people fall roughly into three groups: the people of the Columbia Plateau, the Basin, and the coast.

Nez Perce women and their mat-covered dwellings, called longhouses

PEOPLE OF THE COLUMBIA PLATEAU

Forests and streams provided food for the people of the Columbia Plateau. They harvested salmon and other fish, and hunted elk, deer, and smaller game. In order to create grazing areas for game, they set fire to the forest undergrowth. This practice created open grasslands and forests of fire-resistant trees such as oak and ponderosa pine.

Many nations lived in the Columbia Plateau, including Umatillas, Nez Perces, Cayuses, and Klamaths. For part of the year, they lived in villages. At other times, they packed up their belongings and moved to hunting grounds. Everyone worked hard for the group's survival, and everyone's efforts were valued. Although each group had a chief or headman (or occasionally a headwoman), there was no royalty.

PEOPLE OF THE BASIN AND RANGE

Northern Paiutes lived in Oregon's Basin and Range Region, the most barren part of the state. An unending search for food shaped their lives. People hunted small game such as rabbits and birds, and killed deer when they could find them. Women and children gathered seeds, roots, and berries. They also caught crickets and grasshoppers, a rich source of protein that they ate raw or fried.

Northern Paiutes never stayed in one place for very long. They moved every few months, always heading toward a new food supply. In the spring, they went to places where they could collect edible seeds and roots. In summer, they spread out to gather and dry crickets, berries, and more seeds. In summer and fall, the women gathered pine nuts to last through the winter, while the men hunted game. In the winter, when game and other food were hard to find, the people lived in tiny huts made of willow branches. They lived on the food they had stored and waited for spring to come again.

A Paiute water basket

PEOPLE OF THE COAST

Many different Native American groups lived along the coast of Oregon by 1790. Among the nations were the Chinook, the Clatsop, and the Tillamook.

The coastal peoples lived in a land of abundance. The ocean and rivers gave them all the fish and shellfish they could eat. Because they rarely had to worry about finding food, the coastal people had time to develop arts such as dance, carving, canoe building, and storytelling. The Wasco people, who lived along the Lower Columbia River, shared many characteristics of the coastal cultures because they too had an abundant food source—salmon.

The coastal people generally lived in towns or villages, in houses built of cedar planks, supported by a framework of poles. Some houses were as long as 100 feet (30 m) and sheltered several families. Sleeping platforms stood on posts about 5 feet (1.5 m) above the ground. Families stored food, clothing, pottery, and other things in the space underneath.

Clatsops, Chinooks, and other coastal peoples traveled up and down the rivers and along the coast in canoes made from hollowed-out logs. One early white visitor wrote with admiration, "Their canoes are made of cedar, and although [they] possess no other instrument than a small chisel, it would be in vain for any white (with every tool he could wish) to set up a competition with them in this art; if perfect **symmetry**, smoothness, and proportion constitute beauty, they surpass anything I ever beheld."

As time passed, some people in the coastal towns gathered more wealth and power than others. Eventually, the people of these groups fell into three social classes. The chiefs and their extended families formed the richest and most powerful class. Custom allowed a chief to have several wives.

Scientists estimate that on average, the Native Americans along the Oregon coast ate 365 pounds (166 kilograms) of salmon per person per year, or 1 pound (0.45 kg) of salmon a day!

Q8 HOW DID THE COASTAL PEOPLE CATCH SALMON?

A8 Most salmon fishing was done with large nets, or seines. One seine could be 16 feet (5 m) wide and as much as 600 feet (180 m) long! Heavy stones held down one end and wooden floats kept the other end on the water's surface. The net formed a standing wall in the water. Any fish that swam into it were trapped.

WORD TO KNOW

symmetry *balance, evenness on both sides*

Salmon fishing in the Columbia River

The largest class consisted of commoners, who fished, hunted, and made canoes. Beneath the commoners were slaves, mostly people who had been captured in warfare with other nations. Few in number, enslaved people were largely seen as symbols of wealth for their owners and weren't heavily relied on for their labor. Sometimes, enslaved people were used as trade goods. Traded from one people to another, slaves might travel hundreds of miles from their original home.

WORDS TO KNOW

breechcloths *garments worn by men over their lower bodies*

obsidian *jet-black volcanic glass*

DRESS AND ADORNMENT

Coastal women wore skirts made of animal skins or woven from strips of cedar bark. The skirt hung from the woman's waist by a leather belt and reached below her knees. Men wore skin **breechcloths** wrapped around the waist and thighs. Both men and women pierced their noses. Some jewelry was made from **obsidian** and other stones that came from as far away as Mexico.

Among certain Native peoples, it was common for a mother to strap a pair of boards to her baby's forehead soon after it was born. Pressing on both the top and bottom of the child's head, the boards gradually flattened the soft bone of the child's skull.

This painting shows a Chinook woman holding her baby in a head-flattening board.

ARTS AND LEISURE

Coastal Native Americans carved figures of humans and animals out of wood and bone. They also carved designs of birds, animals, and plants on the posts of their houses and the handles of knives and chisels. Sometimes even the sides of canoes were decorated with carvings.

Dancing was a favorite entertainment of the coastal people. Women and men each danced in their own group. Dances could be graceful and solemn or wild and exciting. A drummer or flute player made music for the dancers to follow.

The coastal people loved to play games of chance. In one game, someone tossed a wooden disk. People made bets over which side would show when the disk landed. Sometimes, the stakes got higher and higher as the game went on. Players would lose canoes, houses, and slaves in the betting. Men could even lose their wives!

Storytelling was a favorite pastime. It was often done in the evenings or at special feast times. Some stories told of disasters that had befallen the group, such as floods or fires. Some described the deeds of great hunters or warriors. Other stories were based on the people's beliefs about the creation of the world. These stories described how the earth was made, how the sun came to be in the sky, and why the fish and forest animals behaved as they did. These stories reflect the close connection between Oregon's first people and the natural world.

RELIGION

Oregon's Indians believed that powerful spirits ruled the natural world. Animals, rocks, plants, clouds, and the sun and moon all had spirits that could affect the lives of human beings. Because humans depended on nature for survival, they wanted to keep the spirits happy. When a hunter killed an elk or deer, he said a prayer to its spirit. He thanked it for dying and asked for others of its kind to come to the hunters as well.

Many rules, or **taboos**, surrounded the killing of game and preparation of food. For example, in some areas, when a young hunter killed his first deer he could not eat it himself. Instead, he was required to offer the meat to the elderly people of the village. Among some groups, meat had to be cut up and cooked in specific ways.

THE HUNTER AND THE ELK SPIRIT

Wascos told the story of a young hunter who met the spirit of the elk. The elk promised to be the young man's guardian, as long as he never killed more elk than he needed. For a time, the hunter was successful and brought plenty of meat back to the village. But his father complained that he should bring even more food. The young hunter set out and killed five whole herds of elk! Seeing this, the elk spirit declared he would no longer be the hunter's guardian. The hunter returned to his village and died in despair.

WORD TO KNOW

taboos *rules about how activities such as hunting and preparing food must be performed*

Picture Yourself . . .

in a Chinook Village

All morning you have been waiting at the river's edge. Again and again you look upstream, but there is no sign of the canoes that will bring the fishermen. You help your mother and the other women tend the cooking fires, and listen to the talk about the salmon runs of past years. "Someday the salmon won't come back," grumbles one old grandmother. "The way people behave these days, the salmon spirit is going to get angry and punish us all!"

Suddenly, you hear a shout and the rhythmic swish of paddles. You rush with the others to the riverbank and watch the canoes gliding toward you. They are heavy in the water, laden with the day's catch. You know that the salmon spirit is happy and your people will have plenty of food for another year.

FAQ

Q8 WHAT WERE SOME TABOOS?

A8 Taboos of all types varied from place to place. Here are a few about catching salmon: A fisherman must not jump or step over the net. He must not cut up the first-caught salmon of the year until the afternoon. Murderers, people who prepare corpses for burial, widows, and widowers must not eat the first catch of the season.

Taboos could be very complex, and they varied from one village to another. Underlying many of these taboos was the belief that humans relied on nature and should be respectful of it.

HOOFPRINTS ON THE GRASSLANDS

In the late 1680s, bands of horses escaped from Spanish settlements in northern New Mexico. The horses found excellent grazing on the grassy plains, and their numbers quickly increased. In the next few decades, they spread northward. By the 1720s, they reached the Columbia Plateau.

It didn't take the Indians long to discover that horses were useful and valuable. Nez Perces, Cayuses, and Umatillas became expert at catching, taming, and riding horses. On horseback, they could travel great distances for trade and warfare. A man who owned many horses was wealthy and admired. As some men acquired more and more horses, while others had few, there was a greater gap between rich and poor within a community. The introduction of horses made villages more vulnerable to raids by other Native peoples. It was difficult to defend against a quick-striking attack by horseback.

The arrival of horses brought great changes to the people of eastern Oregon. Yet few could imagine the far greater changes that lay ahead.

A Nez Perce man on horseback

THE WOMAN WHO SAW THE WHITE MEN

Watkuweis (mid-1700s–early 1800s) grew up in a Nez Perce village. Blackfoot or Atsina warriors from areas to the east captured her and sold her to a white trader. Eventually, she married a white man. When Watkuweis made her way back to Nez Perce land many years later, she told them about the people who had been kind to her. When the first white visitors reached Oregon and met with the Nez Perce people in 1805, they received a warm welcome.

READ ABOUT

The Fur Trade 36

The Corps of Discovery 38

The Astoria Adventure. . . . 41

Westward Movement. . . . 42

Oregon Becomes American 46

This painting depicts the *Golden Hind*, the ship that Sir Francis Drake sailed up the Pacific coast.

1543

A Spanish ship sails up the Pacific coast, possibly to what is now southern Oregon

1792 ▲

Robert Gray becomes the first American to see the mouth of the Columbia River

1805–06

Lewis and Clark spend the winter at Fort Clatsop near the mouth of the Columbia River

EXPLORATION AND SETTLEMENT

★

AROUND 1543, A SPANISH SHIP SAILED ALONG THE COAST OF CALIFORNIA AND MIGHT HAVE REACHED SOUTHERN OREGON. However, the captain did not explore any farther. In 1577, British captain Sir Francis Drake sailed from England, reaching the Pacific Northwest in 1579. He did not explore the area much either, seeing what he described as "vile, thicke, and stinking fogges." Still, he claimed the Pacific lands north of California for England.

1811
Fort Astoria becomes the first permanent U.S. settlement on the Pacific coast

1840s ▲
Thousands of people travel to Oregon along the Oregon Trail

1848
Oregon Territory is formally established.

Exploration of Oregon

The colored arrows on this map show the routes taken by explorers and pioneers between 1775 and 1830.

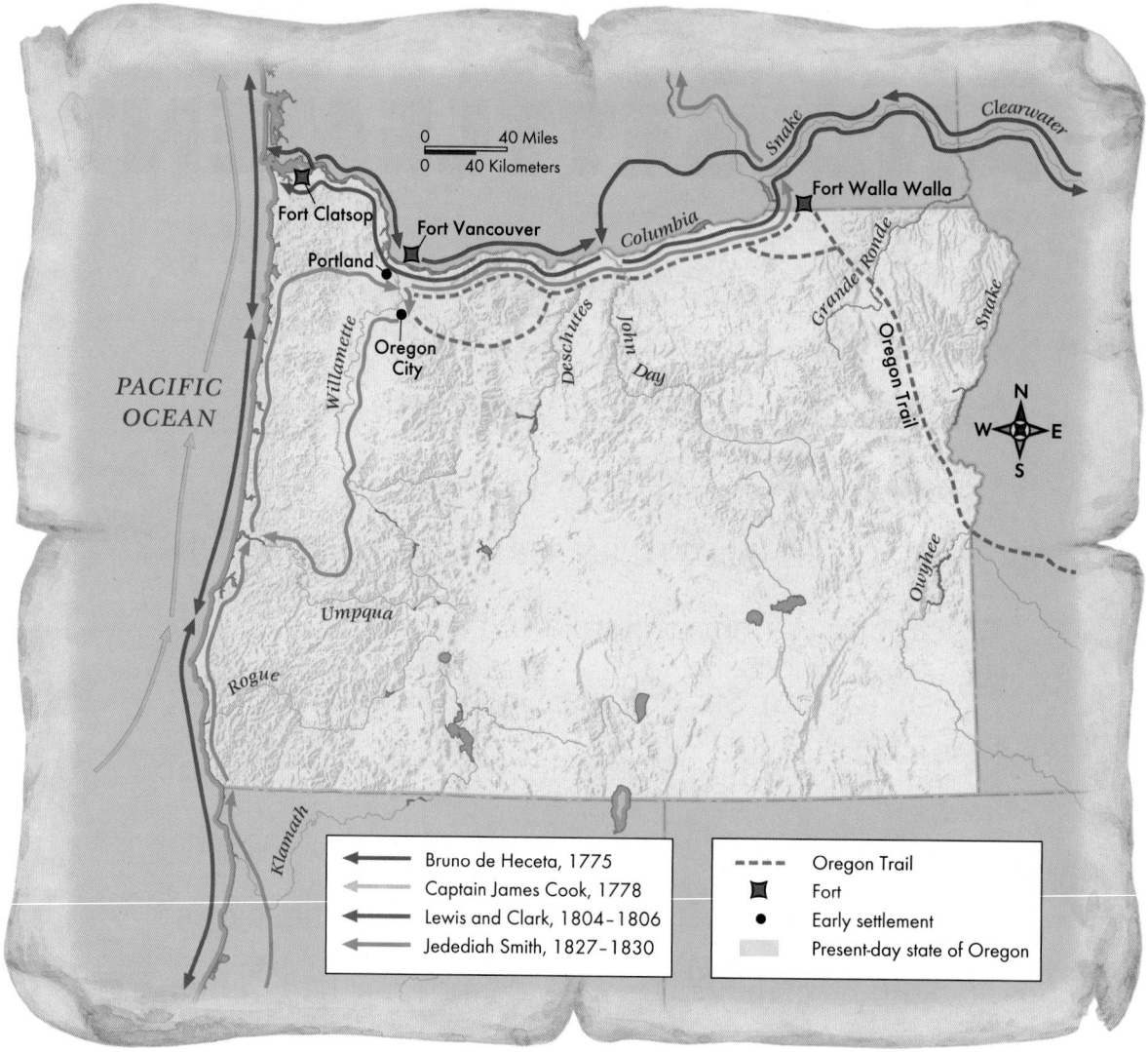

THE FUR TRADE

At first, Europeans paid little attention to Oregon because it did not seem to offer anything they wanted. That suddenly changed in the late 1700s, when Chinese merchants began paying high prices for sea otter pelts. Russians hunted and

Fur trading at Fort Nez Perce

traded for these pelts with the Native people of Alaska and sailed their cargoes across the Pacific to China. Oregon was rich in sea otters, and soon British traders were encouraging Indians in the area to trade the glossy otter pelts for guns, kettles, beads, blankets, and rum.

Back east, the United States was also eager to trade with China. In 1787, the first American merchant ships left Boston, Massachusetts, for China. They sailed all the way around the southern tip of South America and then up the Pacific coast. They stopped at Oregon and Washington to trade for fur pelts before heading across the Pacific.

In 1788, the British North West Company began establishing trading posts in what is now British Columbia, Canada. Indians brought furs to the trading posts and

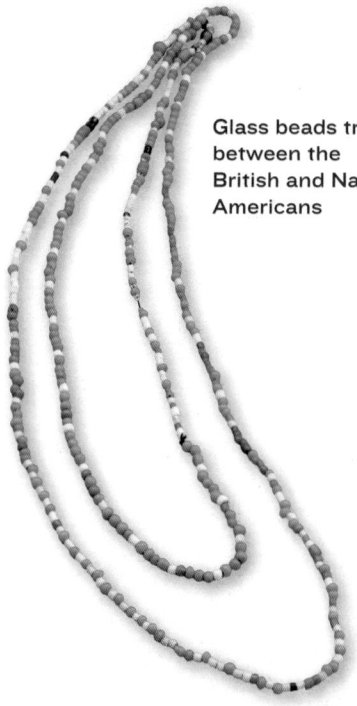

Glass beads traded between the British and Native Americans

exchanged them for guns and other goods. The sea otter trade transformed life for many coastal people. Young men became more focused on otter hunting. The task could be dangerous. One British trader wrote, "Sometimes [Indians] surprise [the sea otter] sleeping on his back, on the surface of the water; and, if they can get near the animal without awakening him, . . . he is easily harpooned and dragged to the boat, when a fierce battle very often ensues between the otter and the hunters, who are frequently wounded by the claws and teeth of the animal."

Hunters slaughtered sea otters in staggering numbers. In just one year, between 1801 and 1802, traders shipped some 14,000 pelts to China from the North Pacific coast. As a result of overhunting, sea otters began to disappear from the Oregon coast. There was still a demand for pelts, so fur traders encouraged the Indians to trap minks, foxes, river otters, and muskrats. Beaver colonies thrived in Oregon's inland forests and streams. Beaver soon replaced sea otter as Oregon's most treasured pelt. And, like the sea otter, the beaver began to disappear.

Robert Gray

A MIGHTY RIVER

In 1792, a Boston-based merchant and sea captain named Robert Gray sailed up the Oregon coast, exploring inlets and bays. During his explorations, he came across a great river emptying into the sea. He named it the Columbia, after his ship, the *Columbia Rediviva*. No river in the Americas dumps more water into the Pacific Ocean than the powerful Columbia. Ironically, Gray was not impressed by what he saw. In his log, he wrote that the river was "not . . . worthy of more attention."

THE CORPS OF DISCOVERY

For more than a century, France had claimed the land from today's Louisiana to the Dakotas and Montana. In 1803, President Thomas Jefferson bought this land in a $15 million deal known as the Louisiana Purchase. With the Louisiana Purchase, the size of the United States had suddenly doubled.

Jefferson was eager to learn about the territory and to establish claims to the land still farther west. In 1803, he picked a Virginia army officer, Meriwether Lewis, to head an exploring expedition. Lewis asked a fellow army officer, William Clark, to help lead the expedition. They recruited many men along the Ohio River on America's western fron-

Sacagawea with explorers Meriwether Lewis and William Clark

tier to join them in what was called the Corps of Discovery. To this band of 33 explorers was later added Sacagawea, a young Shoshone woman. She spoke several American Indian languages. She served as ambassador when the Corps of Discovery met northwestern Native peoples, many of whom provided vital assistance to the expedition.

Jefferson had instructed Lewis and Clark to follow the Missouri River west and to search for a reliable and easy, as well as preferably all-water, route to the Pacific. They followed the Missouri River to its source on today's Montana-Idaho border. From there, they followed the Clearwater and Snake rivers, and finally reached the Columbia. In December 1805, the Corps of Discovery built a rough fort near the mouth of the Columbia. The explorers spent the winter at this fort, which they named Fort Clatsop.

Lewis and Clark made careful notes about the site's relentless fog and rain. During their three-month stay, they had only six days of sunshine! To add to their misery, their clothes and bedding were alive with fleas; many men came down with flu-like illnesses that lasted for months; and, during the winter, elk and pemmican were just about the only things to eat. Out of desperation, they tried another dish: dog meat. Clark disliked it, but Lewis wrote in his journal, "I think it an agreeable food and would prefer it vastly to lean venison or elk."

Despite their troubles and their disappointment in not finding an all-water route, Lewis and Clark returned with glowing reports about Oregon's promise. It was rich in furs, fish, and timber, and the grasslands of the Willamette Valley looked like perfect farming country.

A view of Astoria, at the mouth of the Columbia River, established by John Jacob Astor's Pacific Fur Company

THE ASTORIA ADVENTURE

In 1810, John Jacob Astor, a rich New York businessman, founded the Pacific Fur Company. He sent two expeditions to the Columbia River, one by land and the other by sea. When the oceangoing expedition reached Oregon in 1811, eight crew members drowned in high seas at the mouth of the Columbia River. The survivors awaited the overland expedition. Finally, in early 1812, the first weary members of the overland expedition arrived.

Astor's men built a trading post called Astoria at the mouth of the Columbia. Indians arrived with furs, eager to trade with the newcomers. Just as things seemed to be going well, the Astorians learned that the United States and Great Britain were at war and that a British warship was on the way to attack them! Low on supplies and poorly armed, they knew they could not hold out against the British. The Pacific Fur Company sold its property to the British North West Company, which took over Astoria and renamed it Fort George. Astor, however, continued trading furs through his American Fur Company, based on the East Coast. This became one of the largest fur companies in the country.

Over the next several years, Fort George changed hands a number of times and was controlled by a succession of three different fur trading companies. Eventually, the Hudson's Bay Company began turning a huge profit at the fort. In exchange for furs, the company brought manufactured goods to Native villages along the Pacific coast and up to Alaska. The company also operated a lumber mill and began clearing land throughout the region. Next, the Hudson's Bay Company established Fort Vancouver along the Willamette and Columbia rivers. Slowly, the Chinooks and Clatsops found their homes and their lives to be changing.

John Jacob Astor

Astoria was the first permanent U.S. settlement on the Pacific coast.

CAPTURING THE MOMENT

As European and American settlers moved into Oregon, painters tried to capture the beauty of the land and the experiences of the people. During the 1840s, English artist Henry Warre painted detailed pictures of the settlement at Oregon City. John Mix Stanley painted a portrait of John McLoughlin, the "Father of Oregon." Stanley pioneered the use of photography to capture the changing lives of Oregon's Indians. Historic themes also inspired sculptor Alice Cooper. Her bronze statue of Sacagawea stands today in Portland's Washington Park.

MINI-BIO

JOHN McLOUGHLIN: THE "FATHER OF OREGON"

John McLoughlin (1784–1857) grew up in Canada and studied medicine as a young man. He served as a doctor at a fur-trading post and then became a trader himself. In 1824, he moved to the Oregon country to serve as head trader of the British-owned Hudson's Bay Company. His position afforded him power, and he aided wagon-train settlers in the Willamette Valley and helped keep the peace between Americans and British. In 1957, the Oregon legislature gave McLoughlin the honorary title, "the Father of Oregon."

Want to know more? Visit www.factsfornow.scholastic.com and enter the keyword **Oregon**.

This painting, *The American Village*, by Henry Warre, depicts Oregon City in 1849.

WESTWARD MOVEMENT

In 1811, a clerk with the Pacific Fur Company wrote a glowing description of the Willamette Valley, saying that the climate was "remarkably mild" and the valley possessed "a rich and luxuriant soil, which yields an abundance of fruits and roots." A few years later, a U.S. House of Representatives report claimed that the Willamette Valley was "a boundless extent of the most fertile soil on this continent."

By the 1830s, the young nation was expanding westward. Plows had cut furrows across Indiana, Illinois, and Iowa. Many Americans believed that the nation was meant to spread across the continent all the way to the Pacific Ocean. They said that God wanted the United States to stretch from sea to sea. Some politicians seized on this idea, called Manifest Destiny, and used it to encourage westward expansion.

In 1834, a young Methodist minister named Jason Lee traveled west from Missouri to the Willamette Valley. He intended to bring Christianity to the Indians. Lee worked eagerly. He set up a church and a one-room school near a village of the Kalapuya Nation. But Indian men and women had their own religion and many were not interested in the Bible. Lee traveled back to the East Coast to recruit help. He returned with a group of teachers, ministers, and doctors known as the "Great Reinforcement." They set up branch **missions** at The Dalles and in what is now northwestern Oregon.

While the **missionaries** worked to convert Kalapuyas, the Indians were dying of European diseases. For thousands of years, the people of the Pacific Northwest had had little contact with outsiders. Europeans brought new diseases, such as smallpox, measles, and typhoid. Native Americans had no natural **immunity** to fight these deadly diseases, which swept through village after village. Indians knew of many plants with healing powers. They tried them all, but nothing seemed to help. European diseases wiped out whole towns and villages. Historians believe that between 1770 and 1865, 80 to 90 percent of Oregon's Native people died of disease.

As time passed, the missionaries became less concerned with teaching the Bible and more interested in farming. As their plows broke the land, the missionaries helped prepare the way for thousands of others who would follow. Most 19th-century Americans lived on farms. To them, few things were more valuable than good

Jason Lee

WORDS TO KNOW

missions *places created by a religious group to spread its beliefs*

missionaries *people who try to convert others to a religion*

immunity *natural protection against disease*

Emigrants Crossing the Plains, an oil painting by Albert Bierstadt

soil. Stories of the rich land in the Willamette Valley filled them with excitement.

By the 1840s, many farmers in the Midwest were lured by the promise of the Oregon country. Thousands sold their farms and packed up their belongings. They bought oxen and wagons and joined the stream of **emigrants** heading west. The emigrants traveled with their cows, horses, chickens, pigs, and dogs. There were so many wagons that the wheels ground tracks into the earth that could be seen for the next 100 years.

Emigrants followed a route called the Oregon Trail, traveling along rivers, across plains, and over mountains. They followed the Missouri, the Platte, and the Sweetwater rivers, before turning northwest along the Snake River. At last, they crossed the Blue Mountains in northeastern Oregon and then followed the Columbia. At The Dalles, they boarded rafts for the several-mile trip

WORD TO KNOW

emigrants *people who leave their homes to live in another land*

SEE IT HERE!

BARLOW TRAIL

Following the Oregon Trail with his family, Sam Barlow looked for a shortcut to avoid a raft trip down the Columbia. He discovered a route around the base of Mount Hood. Parts of the road were rough, and in one spot, wagons had to go down a steep slope. Barlow created a "wagon chute" lined with tree stumps. Ropes tied to the stumps were used to lower the wagons slowly. Today, you can hike what's now called Barlow Road and see the wagon chute, where some trees still bear the marks of ropes.

into the Willamette Valley, or they followed a toll road around the base of Mount Hood.

It could take six months for people from the Midwest to reach Oregon. Many died of smallpox and other diseases along the way. "It rains and snows," a woman wrote in her diary. "My children gave out with cold and fatigue and could not travel. . . . I was so cold and numb that I could not tell by feeling that I had any feet at all."

The hardships did not end when travelers reached the valley of their dreams. They had to build cabins for themselves and survive on what little food they could find or buy until they harvested their first crops. Lucy Ann Henderson Deady remembered her first winter near present-day Salem, when she was 11 years old: "There was no floor in the cabin, just earth. There was a big fireplace. There was but one room. There was a big chest and Mother filled this nearly

In 1845, about 2,000 white settlers lived in the Willamette Valley. Just 15 years later, that number had soared to 52,000!

Picture Yourself . . .

on the Oregon Trail

You never knew your feet could hurt so much! You've been walking almost all day, except for half an hour this afternoon when you clambered aboard the wagon. As soon as the oxen started climbing the next hill, your father made you get down and walk again. Now the wagons have all come to a stop, the men have unyoked the teams, and you can enjoy the best part of the day. As your mother and the other women set to work cooking supper, you slip away to look for your friend Sarah two wagons ahead. Sarah says she heard the men talking about a shortcut through the mountains. It will get you to the valley in just 10 more days! You prop your aching feet on a rock and wonder how you will walk one more day, let alone 10! Then you hear your mother calling you to help her stir the pot on the fire. You walk back, your feet throbbing with every step. You ask yourself why your family ever left Indiana. The Willamette Valley better be as good as they say!

full with clothing, and [my sister] Betty and I slept in that. . . . We lived on boiled wheat and boiled peas that winter."

The opening of the Oregon Trail had a disastrous impact on Oregon's Native Americans. The thousands of newcomers killed their game and pushed them off their land. Hoping to be left in peace, many Indians abandoned the Willamette Valley for less-desirable areas.

OREGON BECOMES AMERICAN

In 1843, William Overton of Tennessee and Asa Lovejoy of Boston, Massachusetts, began clearing land on the Willamette River, near where it flows into the Columbia. Overton soon sold his share of the claim to Francis Pettygrove of Portland, Maine. Lovejoy and Pettygrove each wanted to name the settlement after their hometowns. In 1845, they held a coin toss to decide the issue. Pettygrove won, and Portland was born. Before long, the town had a sawmill, a hotel, and a newspaper.

Like the sea otters before them, Oregon's foxes, beavers, and other fur-bearing animals were becoming scarce from relentless trapping. By the 1840s, the British-owned Hudson's Bay Company saw that there was no longer much profit in fur trading. At the same time, American emigrants were scooping up land in the Willamette Valley and crowding out the British.

In Washington, voices in Congress shouted that the United States should drive the British from the area known as Oregon Country, today called the Pacific Northwest. They argued that the U.S.-British boundary should be marked at latitude 54° 40' W, which is well into present-day Canada. In 1844, James K. Polk was elected president on the slogan, "Fifty-four forty or fight!"

The British did not believe that Oregon was worth fighting for, so they offered to make a compromise about

LATITUDE AND LONGITUDE

Mapmakers draw grids on many maps and globes to serve as place markers. Longitude lines run north and south. Latitude lines run east and west, parallel to the equator. Each latitude line has a number based on its distance from the equator. The distance between these lines is measured in units called degrees and minutes, noted by the symbols ° and '.

the boundary line. They gave up their claim to what is now the northwestern United States, but did not agree to setting the boundary at 54°40'. Instead, in 1846, British and U.S. officials signed an agreement establishing the 49th Parallel as the border between U.S. territory and British Canada. The U.S. portion of the Northwest was officially organized as the Oregon Territory in 1848. At last, the United States stretched from sea to shining sea.

A frontier town in what is now Oregon

MINI-BIO

JOE MEEK: SPEAKING FOR OREGON

As a young man, Joseph Lafayette Meek (1810–1875) spent more than 10 years roaming the Rocky Mountains, buying furs from the Indians. Eventually, he married the daughter of a Nez Perce chief and settled near present-day Hillsboro. In 1848, Meek went to Washington and met with President James K. Polk, whose wife was Meek's cousin. He urged Polk to make Oregon a U.S. territory. Meek later served as territorial federal marshal.

Want to know more? Visit www.factsfornow.scholastic.com and enter the keyword **Oregon**.

READ ABOUT

Glittering Dreams.....50

Slavery and Statehood....52

To Market, to Market....52

From Streams to Forests....57

"I Will Fight No More Forever".....60

A view of First Street in Portland, 1880s

1851 ▲
Gold is found in southern Oregon

1851–56
The Rogue River Wars erupt between Indians and white settlers

▲ **1859**
Oregon becomes the 33rd state in the Union

GROWTH AND CHANGE

★

IN 1859, A NEWSPAPER IN PORTLAND LISTED THE SERVICES OF DOCTORS AND LAWYERS, DRUGGISTS AND BLACKSMITHS. Carpenters, masons, and painters clamored for a place in the booming construction business. Dressmakers and dance teachers offered their talents. Oregon was thriving, and Portland was its bustling center.

1861 ▲
Oregon's first railroad opens

1877
The Wallowa band of Nez Perces refuses to move to a reservation

1887
Whites murder 32 Chinese gold miners on the Snake River

Digging for gold along Oregon's southern coast

GLITTERING DREAMS

When Oregon became a U.S. territory in 1848, cash was in short supply. Sometimes, people used bushels of wheat or pounds of sugar as money.

Then thrilling news reached the Willamette Valley. A sawmill overseer had discovered gold nuggets in northern California! Oregon farmers walked away from their plows and their half-tilled fields. The treasure of the Willamette Valley was nothing compared to the riches they imagined in the goldfields to the south.

By the end of 1848, about two-thirds of the white men in Oregon had left for California. Some of them struck it rich and returned with thousands of dollars in their pockets. Oregon's cash shortage was at an end. Instead of wheat and sugar, Oregonians began using gold dust as money. The territory even minted its own five- and ten-dollar gold coins with a picture of a beaver on the back. People called them Oregon Beavers.

In 1851, Oregon experienced a gold rush of its own. A major find was made in the Rogue Valley on Josephine Creek in southern Oregon. Another strike occurred months later at nearby Jackson Creek. Loose gold nuggets were even found on the beaches south of Coos Bay. Hundreds of people joined the rush to the region in hopes of striking it rich.

American trading ships arriving in Chinese ports brought news that gold had been found in California. Before long, throngs of Chinese men flocked there to find jobs in the goldfields. When gold was found in Oregon, hundreds of Chinese people in California pulled up stakes and headed to the Oregon Territory. Many worked in "dead," or unproductive, fields abandoned by white miners.

Oregon farmers produced wheat and other crops that gold miners needed.

SLAVERY AND STATEHOOD

Oregon was a U.S. territory, but it was isolated from the country to which it belonged. Newspapers might be several months old by the time they reached Portland. Nevertheless, Oregonians were keenly aware that the issue of slavery was dividing the country. For most white Southerners, slavery was an accepted part of life. Many people in the North, however, thought that slavery was unfair. They objected to how enslaved people were treated. There was also a concern that farmers who did not own slaves could not compete with landowners who were able to farm on a larger scale by using enslaved laborers. Most Oregonians opposed slavery because of the disadvantage it created for small-scale farmers and wanted it to be forbidden in the territory.

In 1857, the U.S. Supreme Court heard a case concerning an enslaved man named Dred Scott. In the Dred Scott decision, the Court ruled that Congress could not outlaw slavery in a U.S. territory. The only way Oregonians could keep slavery out was to apply for statehood.

In February 1859, the U.S. Congress voted in favor of Oregon's application for statehood. On February 14, Oregon became the 33rd state in the Union. The Willamette Valley town of Salem was established as the capital.

From 1861 to 1865, the United States fought the bloody Civil War. It put an end to slavery at last and kept 11 Southern states from permanently breaking away to form their own nation. Oregon sided with the Union but was affected very little by the war itself. Most fighting was far away, on the other side of the Rocky Mountains.

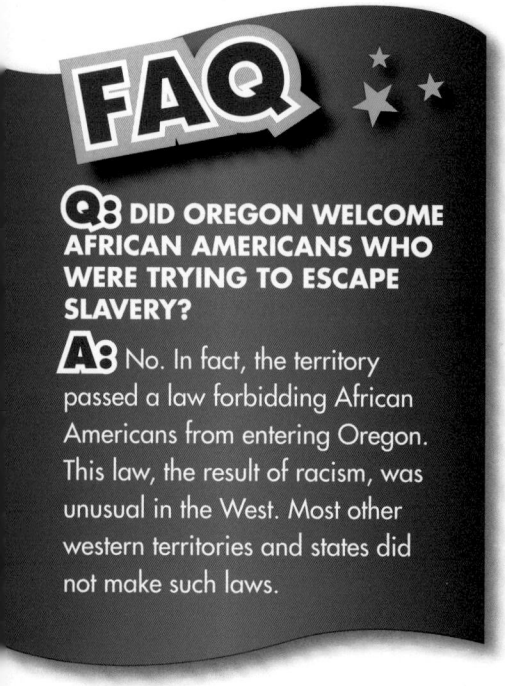

TO MARKET, TO MARKET

The gold rush led to the long-term development of northern California, and San Francisco arose as a major city.

Oregon: From Territory to Statehood

(1848–1859)

This map shows the original Oregon territory and the area that became the state of Oregon in 1859.

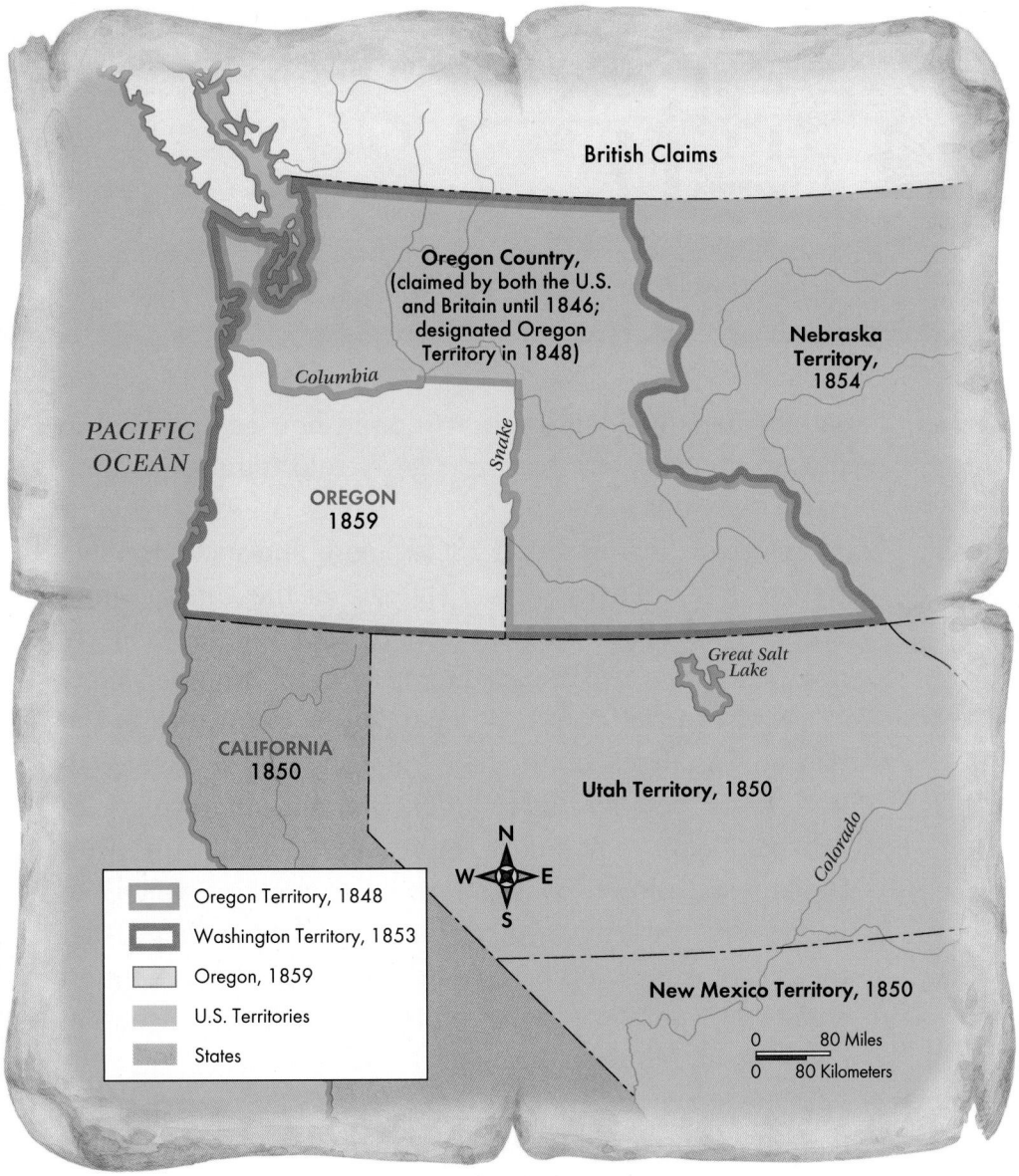

Paddle steamers, like this one on the Columbia River, helped Oregonians get their produce to market.

Californians needed lumber to build houses and food to put on their tables. Oregon eagerly sold Californians the goods they craved.

During the 1850s and 1860s, more and more farmers settled in southern Oregon. The soil of the Umpqua and Rogue river valleys proved excellent for growing wheat. By now, wheat was also the major crop in the Willamette Valley.

Native Americans had depended for centuries on the natural resources of the Umpqua and Rogue river valleys. As farmers poured in and seized this land, American Indians fought to defend it. From 1851 to 1856, American Indians and settlers fought a series of conflicts called the Rogue River Wars. Governor George Curry ordered that the Native Americans be killed on sight. Armed white men attacked American Indian villages, murdering women, children, and men as they slept.

The surviving Indians were eventually driven to the Grand Ronde and Siletz **reservations**. Although officials promised that the reservation land would belong to the

WORD TO KNOW

reservations *lands set aside for Native Americans to live on*

Native Americans forever, the U.S. government whittled away these lands over the years. The American Indians were forced to live in unfamiliar places on poor farmland with little game or fish, and many died.

Until the 1850s, white settlement had not touched most of eastern Oregon. Then the search for gold led whites into the remote reaches beyond the Cascades. They found gold, and miners started moving into the area. Soon farmers realized that cattle and sheep could flourish on the sagebrush and grasses of the high plateau. Herds of steers and flocks of sheep grazed on land that people had once thought unfit for farming, providing food and goods for the miners.

As it grew, Oregon encouraged more people to come and settle. "We can offer the emigrant a civilization fresh in its newness," boasted a Willamette Valley newspaper in 1869. "We have forests for the lumberman of Maine, and fisheries for the fisherman of Cape Cod. . . . We have the soil whereon to settle hundreds of thousands."

In order to get their produce to market, Oregonians needed a speedy, reliable system of transportation. The Willamette, Columbia, and other rivers were natural shipping routes. Steamboat companies cleared and widened river channels so they could handle large vessels. Between 1861 and 1864, the Oregon Steam Navigation Company carried about 100,000 steamboat passengers.

In 1861, Oregonians saw their first railroad locomotives. A short rail line was built to carry goods and passengers overland around the Cascades and Celilo Falls of the Columbia. Below the falls, they could catch a steamboat for the rest of the journey. People across the country cheered in 1869 when the first **transcontinental** railroad was completed. It linked the railway system of the eastern states with California. The trip across the

WORD TO KNOW

transcontinental *crossing an entire continent*

MINI-BIO

HENRY VILLARD: THE MAN WHO BUILT THE RAILROAD

In 1873, Henry Villard (1835–1900), a native of Germany, moved to Portland, where he invested in the Northern Pacific Railway. He became president of the company in 1881. He donated millions of dollars to the newly established University of Oregon at Eugene. Villard also merged several East Coast electric companies. His new company later became General Electric.

Want to know more? Visit www.factsfornow.scholastic.com and enter the keyword **Oregon**.

Rockies once took six months of dangerous and exhausting travel. Now it was reduced to a few high-speed days. In 1883, Portland was linked by rail to the transcontinental line, and this connection made it easier to ship goods from Oregon to many other parts of the United States. And Oregonians could read a newspaper from New York or Philadelphia the very week it was printed!

The Union Pacific Railroad Company brought thousands of men from China to lay down track in California and Oregon. They worked tirelessly on a diet of rice and tea. Yet they received a hostile welcome in the

Laying track for the Union Pacific Railroad

United States. Some white workers accused them of driving down wages. Many Americans mistrusted the Chinese because their language and religion were different. During the 1880s, anti-Chinese gangs drove Chinese laborers out of Portland, Salem, Oregon City, and other towns. In the mid-1800s, many Chinese also came to Oregon to work as miners, but they faced discrimination. One observer wrote that Chinese miners "moved from mining locality to mining locality, fleeing from the kicks of one to the cuffs of another."

In 1887, at least 30 Chinese gold miners died in a cove on the Snake River in eastern Oregon. The miners were murdered by a group of white thieves who believed that the Chinese had struck it rich and buried a treasure near their camp.

MINI-BIO

BETHENIA OWENS-ADAIR: MAKING HER OWN WAY

In 1843, Bethenia Owens-Adair (1840–1926) traveled from Missouri with her family on the Oregon Trail. After running a hat shop in Roseburg for six years, she went to Philadelphia to attend medical school. She returned to Oregon in 1881 and set up a successful medical practice in Portland. A few years later, she moved to Astoria and established her practice there. At that time, very few women worked as doctors. Owens-Adair boldly spoke out for women's rights and argued that women should be allowed to vote.

Want to know more? Visit www.factsfornow.scholastic.com and enter the keyword **Oregon**.

FROM STREAMS TO FORESTS

For thousands of years, salmon provided food for Oregon's Native people. In the years after the Civil War, new Oregonians began to sell salmon for profit. New techniques for preserving and canning fish allowed companies to sell Columbia River salmon to markets as far away as England and Australia. Salmon were caught in huge nets that spanned streams and rivers. In some places, machines called salmon wheels scooped the fish out of the water with giant turning shovels.

MINI-BIO

ROSCOE LEE DIXON: OPEN FOR BUSINESS

In the late 19th century, Oregon laws outlawed African Americans from moving into the state. That didn't stop Roscoe Lee Dixon (1843–?), who arrived from Virginia after the Civil War. He opened a successful business, Roscoe's Oyster House, in Astoria. He was one of the first African Americans to set up a business in the state.

Want to know more? Visit www.factsfornow.scholastic.com and enter the keyword **Oregon**.

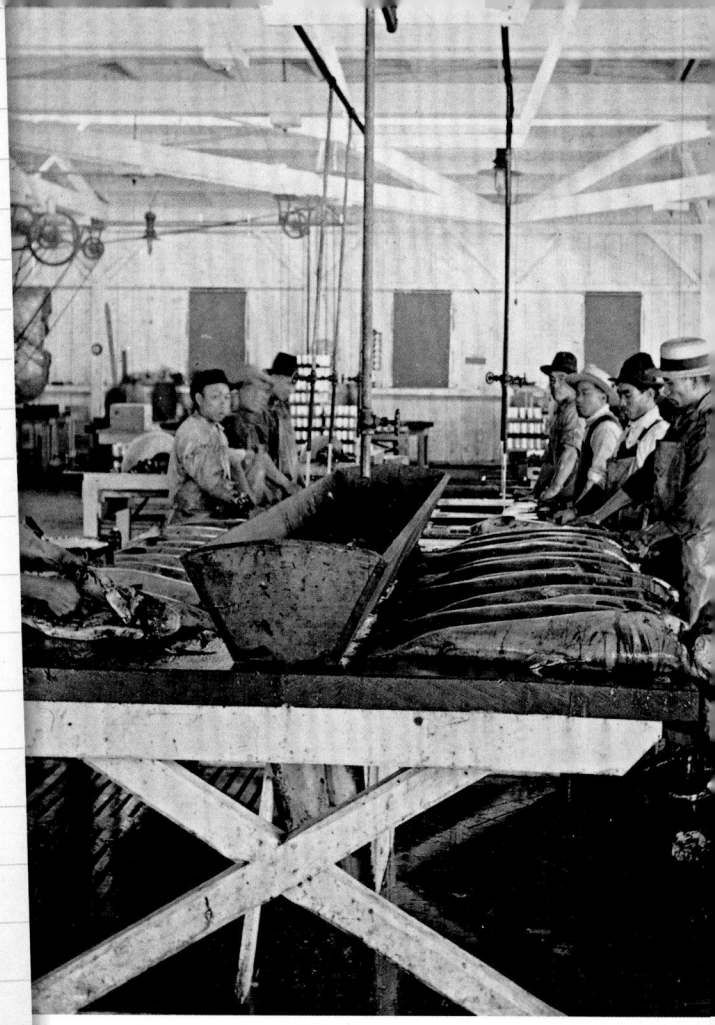

Chinese workers at a salmon cannery near Astoria

WOW

During three months in 1894, a salmon wheel near The Dalles scooped 227,000 pounds (102,965 kg) of fish from the Columbia River.

At salmon-canning factories in Portland, Astoria, and other growing cities, workers packed fresh salmon into 1-pound (0.45 kg) cans. Forty-eight cans were then packed into a single case for shipping. In 1866, Oregon shipped 4,000 cases of salmon. By 1887, that number had zoomed to 620,000!

The intensive fishing quickly depleted the salmon stock in the Columbia and other rivers. In 1894, an Oregon game official wrote, "For a third of a century Oregon has drawn wealth from her streams, but now, by reason of her wastefulness and lack of intelligent provision for the future, the source of that wealth is disappearing."

Oregon's forests proved to be another source of wealth, and new steam-powered technology allowed loggers to work farther away from water during the late 1800s and early 1900s. A steam-powered machine called the donkey engine hauled massive logs of pine and Douglas fir from the woods to nearby railways. Logging was especially heavy along rivers and railroad lines, which carried the raw timber to the sawmills. The mills sliced the logs into lumber to be shipped as far as the eastern United States and Europe.

NATIVE AMERICAN ACTIVIST

Silas B. Smith (1840–1902) had a Clatsop mother and a white father, and he spent a lot of time among the Clatsop people during his early years. As a young man, he attended college, where he earned a law degree. He then set up a law practice in Astoria. He helped Oregon Indians fight to receive payment for their land from the federal government. He also wrote many articles celebrating the history and cultures of Native Americans of the Northwest.

A train transporting newly cut logs from Oregon forests

A battle scene from the Nez Perce War of 1877

"I WILL FIGHT NO MORE FOREVER"

In 1855, a U.S. treaty granted the Nez Perce people a permanent reservation in Wallowa Valley, part of their traditional homeland. But, greedy for the Indians' lush grazing land, white ranchers pressured the government to move the Nez Perce people to a reservation in Idaho. In 1877, the American Indians received word that they would have to move. Many Nez Perce groups chose to live on the Idaho reservation, which was on another part of their traditional homeland. Some bands, whose ancestors had not traditionally lived in that region, refused to go, and violence erupted.

A young chief named Hinmuuttu-yalatlat, or Thunder Rolling Down Mountain, led the Wallowa band of Nez Perces. The whites knew him as Joseph, a name Christian missionaries gave him as a boy. Fleeing from the U.S. Army, Chief Joseph led his people into the mountains. For four months, the army pursued Nez Perces across Idaho and into Montana. Chief Joseph hoped to lead his people across the Canadian border, where the army could not follow them. They were captured only 40 miles (64 km) from the border.

As he surrendered, Chief Joseph gave one of the saddest speeches in American history. "It is cold and we have no blankets," he said simply. "The little children are freezing to death. . . . I am tired. My heart is sick and sad. From where the sun now stands I will fight no more forever."

The Nez Perce War of 1877 was the last major Indian war in Oregon history. White people had taken over much of the region's most valuable land and would shape it to serve their purposes in the coming century.

FAQ

Q8 WHAT FINALLY BECAME OF THE WALLOWA NEZ PERCES?

A8 The army moved Chief Joseph's band to Kansas, then to present-day Oklahoma. In 1885, Chief Joseph and those who remained of his band were returned to the Pacific Northwest. Many of them lived on reservations of other Native groups and never saw the Wallowa Valley again.

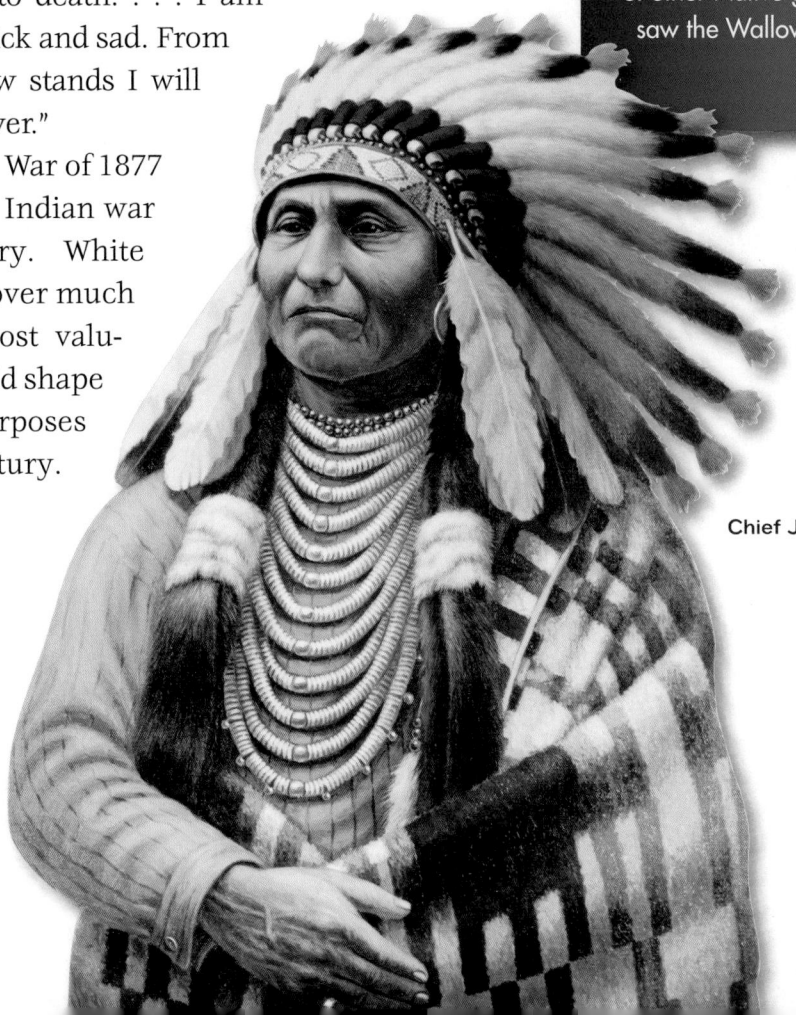

Chief Joseph

READ ABOUT

A Zeal for Reform . . . 64

Wartime and Boom Time . . . 67

Hard Times and Wartime. . . 68

Respecting the Land. 72

A busy Portland street, early 1900s

1902

The Oregon constitution is changed to allow initiatives and referendums on the ballot

▲1912

Oregon women win the right to vote

1923

Oregon bars Japanese immigrants from purchasing land in the state

CHAPTER FIVE

MORE MODERN TIMES

IF YOU WALKED THROUGH PORTLAND IN 1900, YOU MIGHT HAVE HEARD A STREET VENDOR SINGING IN ITALIAN. You might have seen Chinese men talking on a busy corner. You might have seen an African American police officer on duty. You might have heard workers in a salmon-canning factory speaking in Russian. Oregon had become a promised land for people from other parts of the United States and around the world.

1938 ►
The Bonneville Lock and Dam is completed on the Columbia River

1942–45
Vanport becomes the second-largest city in Oregon

2014
Oregon's state minimum wage is raised to $9.10 an hour

A ZEAL FOR REFORM

Some new arrivals found work in the logging, fishing, and ranching industries. Many settled in Portland and took jobs in Oregon's factories and mills. Often they worked for low wages and lived in crowded, unhealthy conditions—while their employers grew wealthy in the railroad, logging, canning, and other industries.

Some Oregonians worked hard to help the state's poor. They opened hospitals and homes to care for orphans. They also challenged the system of voting. As in most states, Oregon voters elected representatives to the state legislature, expecting their representatives to support laws that would benefit the people. In 1902, Oregon changed its

A group of harvest workers resting on sacks of grain

constitution to create a new system. The "Oregon System" allowed people to vote directly on statewide issues in referendums. Voters could also place a possible law on the ballot as an initiative, or plan of action. This example of "direct democracy" proved important to the state and later to the nation.

Through initiatives and referendums, Oregon voters were able to bring about many reforms. They established homes for orphans and hospitals for the mentally ill. Voting soon became complicated as more and more referendums and initiatives were put on each ballot. Referendums and initiatives are still used today, though not as often as they once were.

Another major reform effort carried out in Oregon was one to secure rights for women. In the years after the Civil War, people across the country tried to stop the sale of alcoholic beverages. This was called the temperance movement. In Oregon, women involved with the temperance movement burst into taverns and sang hymns to the customers.

Women realized that they would be better able to change the laws about drinking and other issues if they had the right to vote. In 1871, a former schoolteacher named Abigail Scott Duniway founded a newspaper that championed women's rights (Duniway did not support the temperance movement, but she felt it was important that women have equal rights). The following year, the

MINI-BIO

WILLIAM SIMON U'REN: POWER TO THE PEOPLE

William Simon U'Ren (1859–1949) led Oregonians in the reform movement called populism, which sought to give greater power to the people. In 1902, he fought for and won a constitutional **amendment** that allowed citizens to place initiatives on the ballot and to vote for them directly by referendum. He also helped pass a 1908 amendment that gave voters the power to **recall** elected officials, and he helped establish the first primary election in the nation.

Want to know more? Visit www.factsfornow.scholastic.com and enter the keyword **Oregon**.

WORDS TO KNOW

amendment *a change to a law or legal document*

recall *to remove elected officials from office*

Delegates to the National American Woman Suffrage Association Convention in Portland, 1905

Oregon legislature considered granting **suffrage** to women. The measure lost by only one vote. Oregon passed a law in 1878 that allowed women to own property. Women finally got the right to vote in Oregon in 1912, seven years before an amendment to the U.S. Constitution granted woman suffrage nationwide.

WORD TO KNOW

suffrage *the right to vote*

MINI-BIO

ABIGAIL SCOTT DUNIWAY: A VOICE FOR WOMEN'S RIGHTS

When she was 17, Abigail Scott Duniway (1834–1915) traveled by oxcart with her family from Illinois to Oregon. The long trip west showed her that women often endured the consequences of decisions made solely by men. Later, when she worked as a teacher, she discovered that women were paid far less than men for the same work. She became a local and national leader in the effort to win women the right to vote. Her hard work helped secure the vote for women in Oregon in 1912.

Want to know more? Visit www.factsfornow.scholastic.com and enter the keyword **Oregon**.

WARTIME AND BOOM TIME

In 1917, the United States entered World War I. Warships were in demand to fight the enemy at sea and to transport soldiers and supplies to the battlefields in Europe. Thousands of workers flocked to Portland to work in the shipping industry. Young men from Oregon's farms and factories signed up to fight overseas. When they returned, they brought stories of the world beyond their familiar fields and small towns.

Members of the "Portland Bunch," the 116th Depot Brigade, during World War I

At the end of the war, Oregonians in rural areas still lived much as their grandparents had. A man from Grants Pass remembered how his family built their own log cabin in 1918: "My mother and father had four iron wheels off some old washing machines. We made a crude log hauler and that's the only thing we had to haul those big logs on for the cabin! . . . My mother rived [cut] the shakes [shingles] for the roof as well as the barn and the chicken house."

In the 1920s, technological advancements brought radical changes. For the first time, electricity and running water reached Oregon's small towns and many isolated farms. The first telephone wires stretched above country roads.

Automobiles began to replace horse-drawn wagons. Hundreds of miles of rural roads were paved to make driving easier. When Oregonians got cars, they began to venture farther from home, much as Nez Perces had done when they tamed their first horses. During the 1920s, people drove to Oregon's beaches and mountains for weekend visits. Mountain climbing in the Cascades and Klamaths became a popular pastime.

This photograph shows a gathering of Ku Klux Klan members meeting at the Lane County Rodeo Arena in the early 1920s.

Not all Oregonians enjoyed the good times of the 1920s, however. Oregon was still unfriendly toward many people. The Alien Land Act of 1923 made it illegal for immigrants from Japan to buy land in the state. A white supremacist organization called the Ku Klux Klan spread hatred and sometimes used violence against Catholic immigrants, Asians, Jews, and African Americans. The Klan tried to shut down Catholic schools and to discourage African Americans from settling in Oregon. By 1924, the Klan fell out of favor when Oregonians saw the corruption of its leaders.

HARD TIMES AND WARTIME

In 1929, the New York stock market crashed, throwing the country further into the Great Depression. Banks and factories closed, and millions of people across the country lost their jobs. Oregon farmers had to sell their wheat and beef for a fraction of what they were worth a few years before.

During the Depression, President Franklin D. Roosevelt established government programs called the New Deal to create jobs for thousands of Americans. In Oregon, young men hired by the Civilian Conservation Corps (CCC) developed parkland for public use. (The CCC was not open to women.) The Works Progress Administration hired men and women as writers, artists, and photographers to document Oregon life and history. Most Oregonians welcomed the programs and were glad to have the jobs they created, but some people grumbled that the programs were a waste of money. Oregon governor Charles Henry Martin complained that the country was pampering its people. Martin was not reelected.

In 1937, Japan invaded China, kicking off World War II in Asia. On December 7, 1941, Japanese planes bombed the U.S. naval fleet stationed at Pearl Harbor in the Hawaiian Islands, forcing the United States to enter the war. People in Oregon worried that the Japanese would attack the U.S. mainland next and that the Oregon coast would be a prime target. Many people also feared

SEE IT HERE!

BONNEVILLE DAM

In 1933, the federal government began the Bonneville Lock and Dam, a massive construction project on the Columbia River. Completed in 1938, the dam spans the river 40 miles (64 km) east of Portland at the Columbia River Gorge. The lock and dam generate electrical power for Oregon and Washington, and make it easier for large ships to travel on the lower Columbia. The dam created a large reservoir known as Lake Bonneville. The dam has 18 spillway gates over a length of 1,450 feet (442 m), which allow water to be released. A new lock opened to replace the original one in 1993.

CCC workers planting seedlings on an Oregon hillside in 1939

FAQ

Q8 DID THE JAPANESE EVER ATTACK THE MAINLAND UNITED STATES?

A8 On June 21, 1942, a Japanese submarine lobbed shells at Fort Stevens near the mouth of the Columbia River. The fort was undamaged in the attack. On May 5, 1945, a Japanese bomb carried by a balloon killed a woman and five children who were picnicking near Lakeview in southern Oregon. They were the only civilian casualties of the war on the U.S. mainland.

WORDS TO KNOW

internment camps *places where people are confined, usually during wartime*

segregated *separated from others according to race, class, ethnic group, religion, or other factors*

During World War II, the shipbuilding center of Vanport was the second-biggest city in Oregon.

that Japanese Americans living on the West Coast might be spies for the Japanese government.

In February 1942, President Roosevelt signed an order sending Japanese Americans along the West Coast to **internment camps** farther inland. With only a few weeks' notice, thousands of loyal American citizens were forced to leave their homes, schools, and jobs and placed in camps surrounded with barbed wire. Meanwhile, many young Japanese American men fought in Europe and died for the United States during the war.

World War II helped pull the United States out of the Depression. The government poured vast amounts of money into the military, and the country went back to work making everything from ships to uniforms. Camp Adair near Corvallis became a bustling army training facility. The Kaiser Shipyards near Portland went into high gear. They could turn out a 10,000-ton "liberty ship" in just 10 days. To house the thousands of shipyard workers and their families, the government created Vanport, a community of hastily built cottages north of Portland. Many of the shipyard workers who came to Oregon during the war were African Americans. Despite their hard work, African Americans continued to experience discrimination in the state. Housing in Vanport was **segregated** by race.

BUILDING THE FUTURE

Henry John Kaiser (1882–1967) was born in New York but moved to the Northwest in the early 1900s. In 1914, he started a road-building company, which soon became known for its excellent work. In 1931, he branched out into dam building. His company worked on the Hoover, Grand Coulee, and Bonneville dams. During World War II, Kaiser's company turned to shipbuilding and became a leader in the industry. One of his shipyards was located in Portland. After the war, he expanded into housing construction and built 10,000 new homes.

Another group of workers who arrived in Oregon during the war came from Mexico. Because so many U.S. men were away fighting the war, there was a great need for farmworkers. In 1942, the Mexican Farm Labor Program was begun as a way to bring "guest workers" to the United States. Also known as the bracero program, this system helped with the huge labor shortage. But many of the workers were treated badly and paid poorly. By the time the program ended in 1964, more than 15,000 Mexicans had settled in Oregon.

MINI-BIO

BEATRICE MORROW CANNADY: CHANGING THE LAWS

When Beatrice Morrow Cannady (1890–1974) moved to Portland in 1910, she joined the city's small but active African American community. She and her husband edited the *Advocate*, the city's only African American newspaper. Eventually, she left newspaper work and earned a law degree. In 1925, she worked successfully to repeal Oregon's Black Laws. Dating back to territorial days, these laws said that African Americans could not settle in Oregon. Cannady moved to Los Angeles in the 1930s and lived there for the rest of her life.

Want to know more? Visit www.factsfornow.scholastic.com and enter the keyword **Oregon**.

Mexican laborers picking potatoes in an Oregon field, 1943

Oregonians of all ages protested development of beach areas in 1968.

RESPECTING THE LAND

World War II brought thousands of workers to Oregon. Once the war was over, many decided to live and work in Oregon's towns and cities. The state's natural beauty enchanted many of these new Oregonians. They enjoyed hiking, canoeing, mountain climbing, and other outdoor activities.

In the 1960s and 1970s, Oregon lawmakers acted to protect and restore the environment. New laws limited the amount of logging allowed in state forests and required that new trees be planted. Volunteer crews, including thousands of schoolchildren, planted trees throughout the state.

New dams and irrigation projects brought water to the dry plateaus east of the Cascades. Apple and cherry orchards flourished on land that was once suitable only for grazing sheep and cattle.

In the 1980s, a slowdown in the construction business weakened Oregon's timber industry. Many logging operations and lumber mills shut down. The industry revived somewhat in the 1990s, but many lifelong loggers retired or moved on to other jobs. Many rural areas of the state continue to struggle economically, especially in the wake of the worldwide financial crisis of 2007–2008.

In 2014, Oregon raised the minimum wage workers could be paid to $9.10, one of the highest minimum wages in the nation. Many of these workers are in service industries such as tourism. Tourism in Oregon directly accounts for about 91,000 jobs and creates another 41,000 jobs in related industries. The industry became increasingly important in the 2000s. Today, tourism in the state is a $9.2 billion industry, and much of it occurs in natural areas. Mount Hood, Crater Lake National Park, and Bonneville Dam on the Columbia River are three of the state's major tourist attractions. In recent years, recreational bicycling has attracted thousands of visitors, who come to enjoy Oregon's natural beauty and user-friendly parks and pathways. In 2013, biking contributed about $400 million to Oregon's tourism industry.

Visitors at Fort Clatsop National Memorial, part of the Lewis and Clark National Historical Park

READ ABOUT

Who's an Oregonian?...76

Going to School 80

Works of Beauty.....80

Telling Tales 81

Voices and Images.....83

Taking on Challenges ...85

Music fans gather for the Waterfront Blues Festival in Portland.

PEOPLE

ON AVERAGE, OREGON HAS 40 PEOPLE PER SQUARE MILE (15 PER SQUARE KILOMETER). New Jersey, in contrast, has more than 1,000 people per square mile (458 per sq km). This doesn't mean that most Oregonians live in wide-open spaces. In fact, nearly half of the state's people are packed into and around the city of Portland. Almost 80 percent of all Oregonians live in cities. The rest live on farms or in towns of 2,500 people or less. Most rural people are farmers or ranchers living east of the Cascades.

Where Oregonians Live

The colors on this map indicate population density throughout the state. The darker the color, the more people live there.

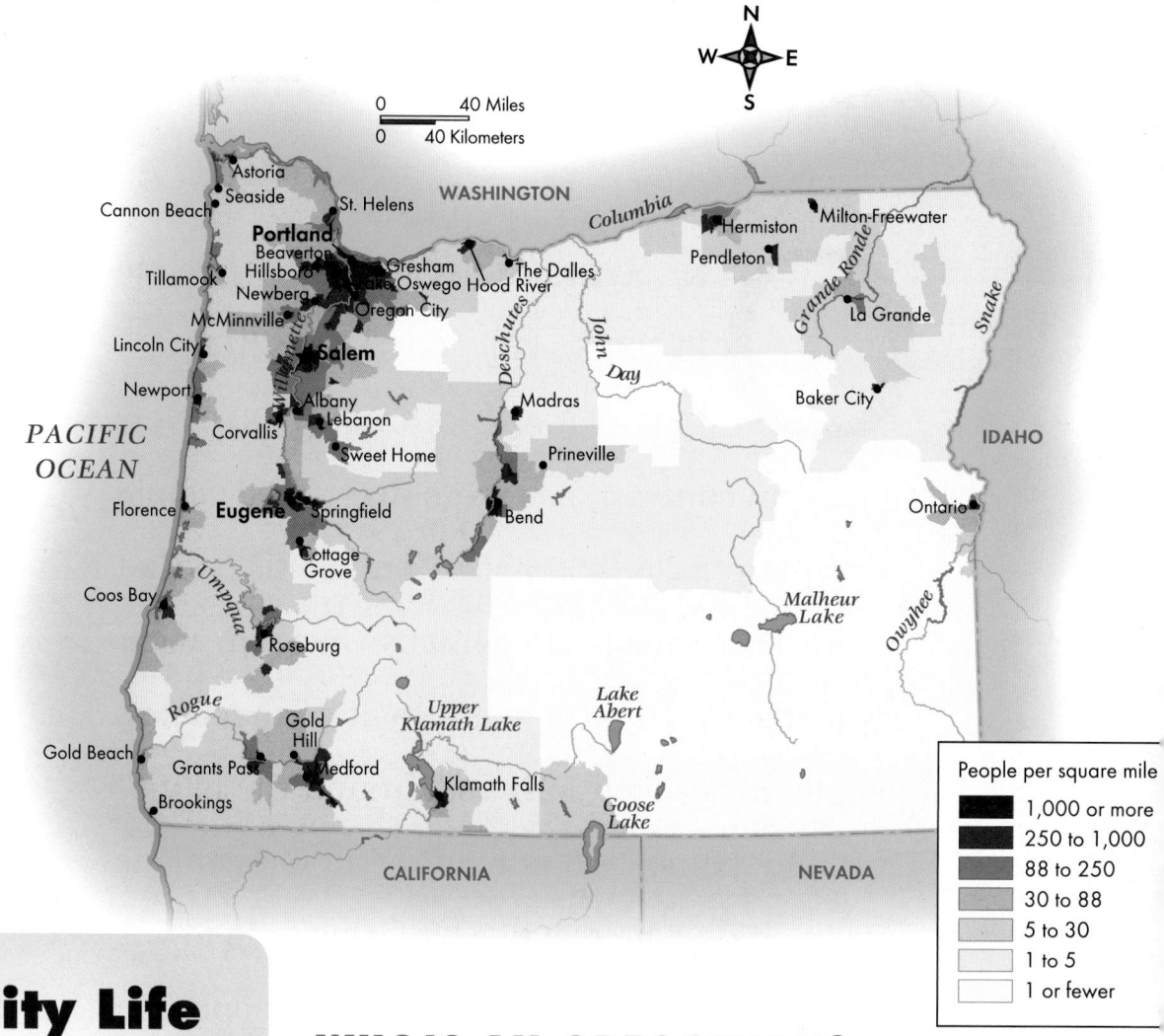

Big City Life

This list shows the population of Oregon's biggest cities.

Portland 583,776
Eugene 156,185
Salem 154,637
Gresham 105,594
Hillsboro 91,611

Source: U.S. Census Bureau, 2010 census

WHO'S AN OREGONIAN?

Oregon values its reputation as a scenic state with friendly, open-minded people. The people of Oregon represent virtually every ethnic group and cultural background. They contribute a rich medley of music, food, arts, crafts, and literature to the state.

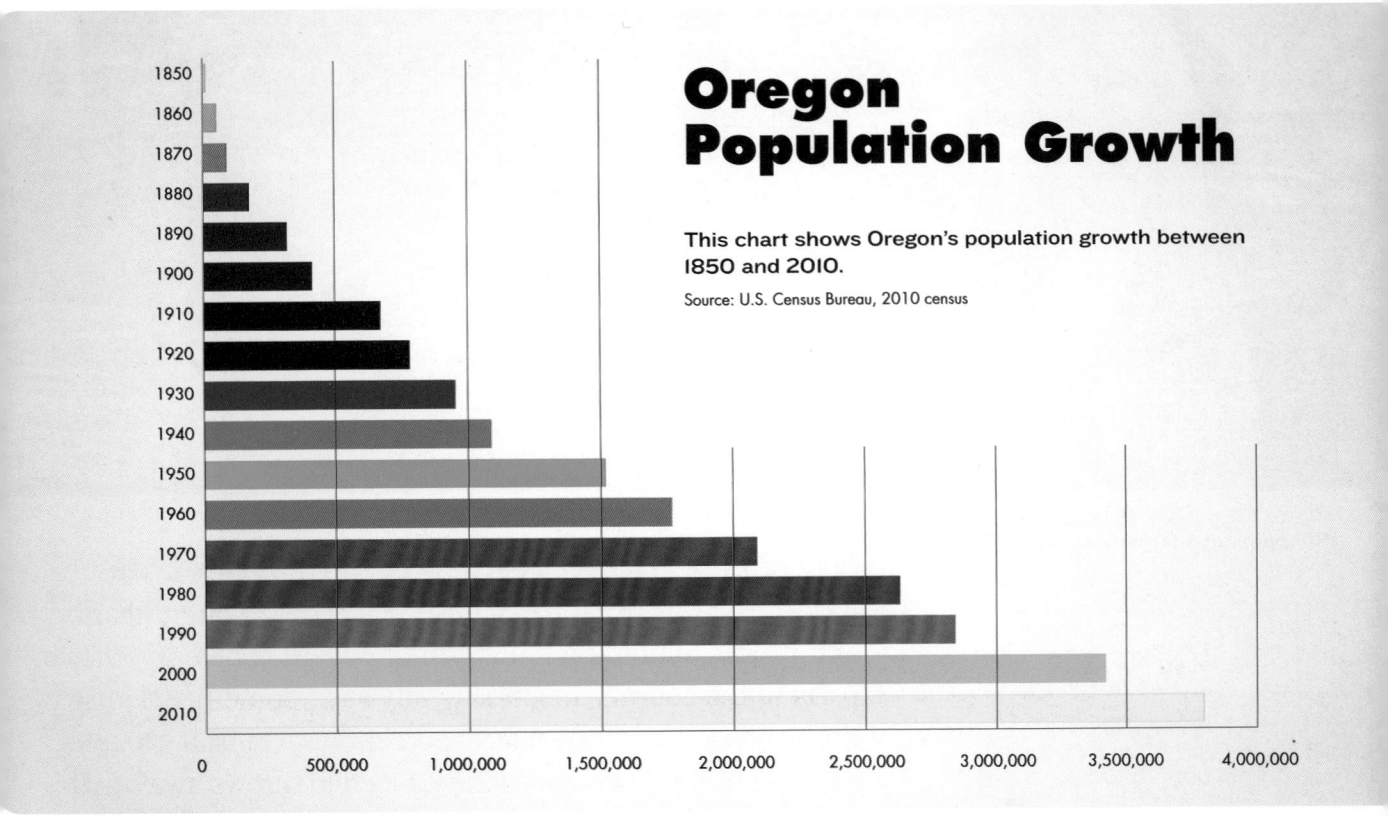
Oregon Population Growth
This chart shows Oregon's population growth between 1850 and 2010.
Source: U.S. Census Bureau, 2010 census
1850
1860
1870
1880
1890
1900
1910
1920
1930
1940
1950
1960
1970
1980
1990
2000
2010
0
500,000
1,000,000
1,500,000
2,000,000
2,500,000
3,000,000
3,500,000
4,000,000

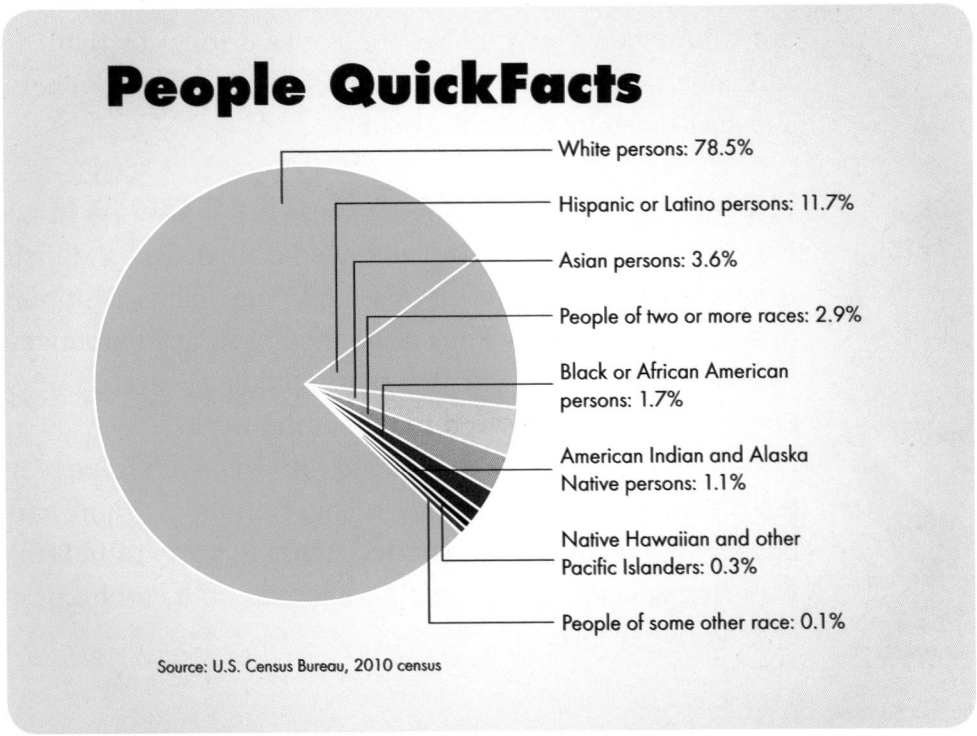
People QuickFacts
White persons: 78.5%
Hispanic or Latino persons: 11.7%
Asian persons: 3.6%
People of two or more races: 2.9%
Black or African American persons: 1.7%
American Indian and Alaska Native persons: 1.1%
Native Hawaiian and other Pacific Islanders: 0.3%
People of some other race: 0.1%
Source: U.S. Census Bureau, 2010 census

Shopping at a farmers market in Eugene

HOW TO TALK LIKE AN OREGONIAN

East of the Cascades, the phrase "I reckon" is often heard, and people tend to say "at any rate" where people in other parts of the country might say "anyway." Some people use the word *necklet* for necklace. Sometimes, colorful phrases slip into ordinary conversation. If a child throws away part of her meal, her grandmother might comment, "You'll see the time when you'll follow the crows a mile for that!" If someone puts on airs, an Oregonian might remark, "There she goes, head up and tail a-risin'!"

Dungeness crab

HOW TO EAT LIKE AN OREGONIAN

For thousands of years, Indians lived on fish and shellfish from Oregon's coast and rivers, and Oregonians continue to savor their seafood. They also enjoy fresh farm products, including hazelnuts, berries, dairy products, and honey. Oregon pears are known throughout the world.

Oregon chefs have developed hundreds of recipes for dishes made with homegrown ingredients. Salmon can be served baked, grilled, or fried, with an array of mouth-watering sauces. The prized Dungeness crab can be purchased live or precooked.

MENU

WHAT'S ON THE MENU IN OREGON?

Carton of blueberries

The Dungeness Crab

Dungeness crabs live along the Pacific coast from Alaska to northern California. On the Oregon coast, they grow to be about 8 inches (20 cm) long. Eating crabs takes patience, as some of the sweetest meat has to be picked out of the shell with tongs and fingers. Don't worry about getting your hands messy—just enjoy the feast!

Seafood chowder

This delicious dish is a thick combo of fish, clams, potatoes, and vegetables.

Cedar plank salmon

Grilling salmon on a plank of red cedar gives it a deep, smoky flavor. The cedar plank is generally moistened for about 24 hours to keep it from burning.

Fresh pear and goat cheese salad

Sliced pears and chunks of goat cheese nestle on a bed of greens. The salad is garnished with nuts and raisins.

Pear and goat cheese salad

TRY THIS RECIPE

Very Berry Cobbler

An array of desserts make use of Oregon's hazelnuts, blueberries, blackberries, and raspberries. Try this one for Very Berry Cobbler (and be sure to have a grown-up nearby to help):

Ingredients:

FILLING

5 cups berries of any combination: raspberries, blackberries, blueberries, boysenberries, or sliced strawberries
⅓ cup sugar
1 tablespoon flour
Splash of lemon juice (optional)

DOUGH

1½ cups flour
1 teaspoon baking powder
¼ teaspoon baking soda
1 tablespoon sugar
4 tablespoons unsalted butter, chilled

Instructions:

1. Preheat oven to 375°.
2. In a 10- or 12-inch glass pie plate, mix the berries, sugar, flour, and lemon juice (if using).
3. Bake for 30 minutes, stirring once. Remove from the oven.
4. To make the dough, stir the flour, baking powder, baking soda, and sugar together in a medium-sized bowl.
5. Grate the butter with a cheese grater and combine into the dough mixture with a fork or with your hands.
6. When the mixture is thoroughly combined, drop it in 6 large spoonfuls over the berries.
7. Bake for 20 minutes.

GOING TO SCHOOL

Under Oregon law, children between the ages of seven and 18 must attend school. Most Oregon children go to public school. Some attend private schools, and a growing number are homeschooled.

Willamette University in Salem held its first classes in 1842. The publicly funded University of Oregon in Eugene and Portland State University are the biggest universities in the state. Other state-supported schools include Oregon State University in Corvallis and Southern Oregon State College in Ashland. Among Oregon's many private colleges are Willamette University in Salem, Lewis & Clark College in Portland, Pacific University in Forest Grove, Reed College in Portland, and the University of Portland.

MINI-BIO

PIETRO BELLUSCHI: DESIGNING HOUSES TO SUIT THE LAND

Soon after World War I, Pietro Belluschi (1899–1994) moved from Italy to the United States. In 1925, he settled in Portland, where he took a job with a leading architectural firm. Belluschi wanted to design buildings that fit Oregon's natural landscape. His wide, low houses, both simple and spacious, represent his Oregon style. Among his best-known buildings are the Portland Art Museum and the library at Reed College. Belluschi taught architecture at the Massachusetts Institute of Technology (MIT) from 1951 to 1973. He spent his final years in Portland, where he was honored for his lasting contributions.

Want to know more? Visit www.factsfornow.scholastic.com and enter the keyword **Oregon**.

WORKS OF BEAUTY

During the 1930s, Harry Wentz of The Dalles painted vivid watercolors inspired by Oregon's mountains and rugged coast. Clayton "C. S." Price painted scenes of horses, cattle, and cowboy life. Both Wentz and Price taught painting at a school sponsored by the Portland Art Association. The Portland Art Museum, which opened in 1892, displays the work of many of the world's finest painters and sculptors.

Marie Watt is a sculptor who lives and works in Portland and taught art at Portland Community College. Part of her series *Blanket Stories* consists of

Elementary students in Eugene get a close look at the skull of an elephant seal.

towers of folded blankets, some of which were traded to the Native Americans by the Hudson's Bay Company in the 19th century.

TELLING TALES

The legendary past of Oregon's first people forms the backdrop for the 1891 novel *The Bridge of the Gods*, by Frederic Homer Balch. In the 20th century, some Oregon writers drew upon the adventures of the state's white pioneers. In his 1935 novel *Honey*

MINI-BIO

BEVERLY CLEARY: INVENTING RAMONA

When she was growing up, Beverly Cleary (1916–) didn't enjoy reading. She longed for books about children like herself and her classmates. In 1950, she began to fill this gap by publishing her first novel for young people, *Henry Huggins*. For more than 50 years, her books about ordinary kids have delighted readers all over the world. Among her best-loved characters are Henry Huggins, his friend Beezus Quimby, and Beezus's little sister, Ramona. Cleary was born in McMinnville and lived in Portland for much of her life. Most of her stories take place on Klickitat Street, a fictional street in an Oregon town. Statues of Ramona, Henry, and Henry's dog, Ribsy, stand today in Portland's Grant Park.

Want to know more? Visit www.factsfornow.scholastic.com and enter the keyword **Oregon**.

MINI-BIO

URSULA K. LE GUIN: CREATING NEW WORLDS

Ursula K. Le Guin (1929–) has the gift of imagination, combined with a desire to help readers reexamine themselves and what's important to them. She grew up in California and moved to Portland in 1958. Many of her novels portray alien cultures, which mirror our own in startling ways. In 1970, her novel *The Left Hand of Darkness* won the Hugo and Nebula awards for fantasy and science fiction. LeGuin is the author of several books for children, including *Catwings* (1988) and *Jane on Her Own* (1999).

Want to know more? Visit www.factsfornow.scholastic.com and enter the keyword **Oregon**.

Jon Krakauer, author of *Into Thin Air*

in the Horn, H. L. Davis describes farming on the high plateau. Mary Jane Carr depicts the lives of pioneer children in her young adult novel *Children of the Covered Wagon*. Don Berry's 1960 novel *Trask* is about a mountain man's quests in the rain forests and rugged headlands of the Oregon coast.

Oregon serves as the setting for two classic novels by Ken Kesey, who grew up in Springfield. *One Flew over the Cuckoo's Nest* (1962) is set in a large state-run institution for the mentally ill. Oregon's logging country is the setting for *Sometimes a Great Notion* (1964).

The poetry of Lawson Fusao Inada reflects the culture of Japanese Americans on the West Coast. Inada, who taught at Southern Oregon University, spent the World War II years in a detention camp, and this experience is conveyed in many of his poems. He was named Oregon's Poet Laureate in 2006.

A deep love of the outdoors inspires many Oregon writers. Barry Lopez reflects on humans and their relationship with nature in three books of essays: *Desert Notes*, *River Notes*, and *Field Notes*. Both children and adults can enjoy his short novel *Crow and Weasel*. Mountain climbing is a passion for Jon Krakauer of Corvallis. His 1997 best seller, *Into Thin Air*, tells the story of a disastrous expedition to scale Mount Everest.

Fred Armisen (left) and Carrie Brownstein (second from left) perform a sketch on their television show *Portlandia*.

Portlandia is a television comedy series set and filmed in Portland. The show often pokes fun at the Pacific Northwest and celebrates the beauty and uniqueness of the city of Portland. The show was created and is written by Carrie Brownstein and former *Saturday Night Live* cast member Fred Armisen. *Portlandia* debuted in January 2011, and won an Emmy Award for outstanding writing.

VOICES AND IMAGES

In the world of comics and cartoons, several Oregonians are among the best known. Mel Blanc of Portland earned the nickname the Man of a Thousand Voices for his perfor-

MINI-BIO

ERNEST HAYCOX: WRITER OF WESTERN TALES

Ernest Haycox (1899–1950) was one of the most successful writers of Old West fiction. He wrote over 300 short stories and more than 20 novels, many which featured action-adventure Western settings with gunfighters and cowboys. Many of his stories appeared in magazines called pulps, which were printed on inexpensive paper with ragged edges. His story "Stage to Lordsburg" was made into the movie Stagecoach, now considered a classic Western film.

Want to know more? Visit www.factsfornow.scholastic.com and enter the keyword **Oregon**.

mances in radio comedies of the 1930s and 1940s. He could sound like a squawking parrot, a whinnying horse, or an old car in need of a tune-up. Blanc went on to do the voices of Bugs Bunny, Tweety Bird, Porky Pig, Barney Rubble in *The Flintstones*, and a host of other cartoon characters.

Matt Groening grew up in Portland and moved to California after he finished college. In 1977, he started a comic-strip magazine that attracted the attention of a TV producer, who invited him to develop a new cartoon show. Groening's series *The Simpsons* began its run on Fox

Matt Groening, creator of *The Simpsons*, with cutouts of his famous characters

TV in 1989. His stories of the Simpson family poke fun at American politics, consumerism, media idols, fashions, and just about everything else! Groening named many of his characters, including Homer and Marge Simpson, after members of his own family. The Simpsons and their friends live in a western town called Springfield, which resembles Springfield, Oregon.

Another Oregon cartoonist who made a name for himself was John Callahan of Portland. At the age of 21, Callahan was injured in a car accident and became **quadriplegic**. Callahan, who died in 2010, drew by holding a pen between his hands. His cartoons found humor in disability and other topics usually thought too sensitive for comedy. He wrote two memoirs: *Don't Worry, He Won't Get Far on Foot* and *Will the Real John Callahan Please Stand Up?*

A number of Oregonians have become famous in the field of music. Obo Addy taught at Lewis & Clark College in Portland for many years, until his death in 2012. Addy was born in Ghana, West Africa, where he learned traditional drumming and chants from his father. He blended Ghanaian traditional music with Western melodies and instruments to create a musical form he called world beat. Addy founded what is now the Odo Addy Legacy Project, an organization that sponsors an annual festival in Oregon.

TAKING ON CHALLENGES

Many Oregonians spend their weekends and vacations hiking, canoeing, mountain climbing, kayaking, or white-water rafting. Others excel in athletics. Danny Ainge of Eugene played with several NBA teams, including the Boston Celtics and the Phoenix Suns. He played with the Portland Trail Blazers from 1990 to 1992. He was inducted into the Oregon Sports Hall of Fame in 1999.

SEE IT HERE!

OREGON SHAKESPEARE FESTIVAL

Every summer, thousands of theater lovers flock to Ashland in southern Oregon for its Shakespeare festival. Costumes and sets look much as they did in the England of Shakespeare's time. Many plays are performed in an outdoor theater with the mountains in the background.

WORD TO KNOW

quadriplegic *totally or partially paralyzed from the neck down*

Obo Addy

American runner Steven Prefontaine leads the pack during a race at the 1972 Summer Olympics.

WOW

While he was at the University of Oregon, Bill Bowerman trained 31 Olympic athletes and 16 runners who ran the 4-minute mile.

Bill Bowerman coached the track-and-field program at the University of Oregon in Eugene from 1948 to 1972, turning it into one of the best track-and-field programs in the world. On a trip to New Zealand in 1962, Bowerman saw people jogging for fun and exercise. He wrote articles and books about jogging when he returned to the United States. Before long, the whole nation was off and running!

One of the most gifted runners Bowerman ever trained was Steven Prefontaine of Coos Bay. Prefontaine, affectionately known as "Pre," won world records in various distance running categories, from 2,000 meters to 10,000 meters. His career was cut short when he died in a car accident at the age of 24 in 1975.

Another outstanding Oregon runner is Mary Decker Slaney. At age 15, "Little Mary Decker" won the 800-meter dash in a competition at Minsk in present-day Russia. Decker Slaney went on to break numerous world records in the early 1980s. In 2003, she was inducted into the U.S. Track & Field Hall of Fame.

Mary Decker Slaney runs a qualifying heat at the 1998 Summer Olympics.

MINI-BIO

TIFFENY MILBRETT: SOCCER SUPERSTAR

Slight in size at 5 feet 2 inches (1.57 m), but big on talent and hard work, Tiffeny Milbrett (1972–) was a star forward on the U.S. women's national soccer team from 1991 to 2006. The team won an Olympic gold medal in 1996 and a silver medal at the 2000 Olympics, in which she was the team's top goal scorer. In 1999, Milbrett and her team won the Women's World Cup championship, with Milbrett once again leading the team in goals scored. Prior to playing for the national team, Milbrett, who grew up in Hillsboro, had an outstanding college soccer career at the University of Portland.

Want to know more? Visit www.factsfornow.scholastic.com and enter the keyword **Oregon**.

READ ABOUT

The Legislative Branch 92

The Executive Branch 93

The Judicial Branch 94

Local Government . . . 94

Newly elected Oregon senators are sworn in at the state capitol in Salem in 2013.

GOVERNMENT

IN 1857, OREGONIANS APPROVED A STATE CONSTITUTION, OR BODY OF LAWS, WHICH STILL GOVERNS THEM TODAY. The legislature can make amendments to the constitution with the approval of the voters. An amendment can also be placed on the ballot and approved directly by the people in an election. This direct voting is permitted because of the tradition of initiatives and referendums, which dates all the way back to 1902.

MINI-BIO

EDITH STARRETT GREEN: EDUCATION FIRST!

Edith Starrett Green (1910–1987) grew up in a family of teachers, and education was important to her all her life. She represented her Oregon district in the U.S. Congress from 1954 to 1974. In Congress, education and women's rights were her main priorities, and she often said that education should be the nation's number-one concern. In 1963, she worked for the passage of a law that would have given women equal pay with men.

Want to know more? Visit www.factsfornow.scholastic.com and enter the keyword **Oregon**.

The state capitol in Salem

Capital City

This map shows places of interest in Salem, Oregon's capital city.

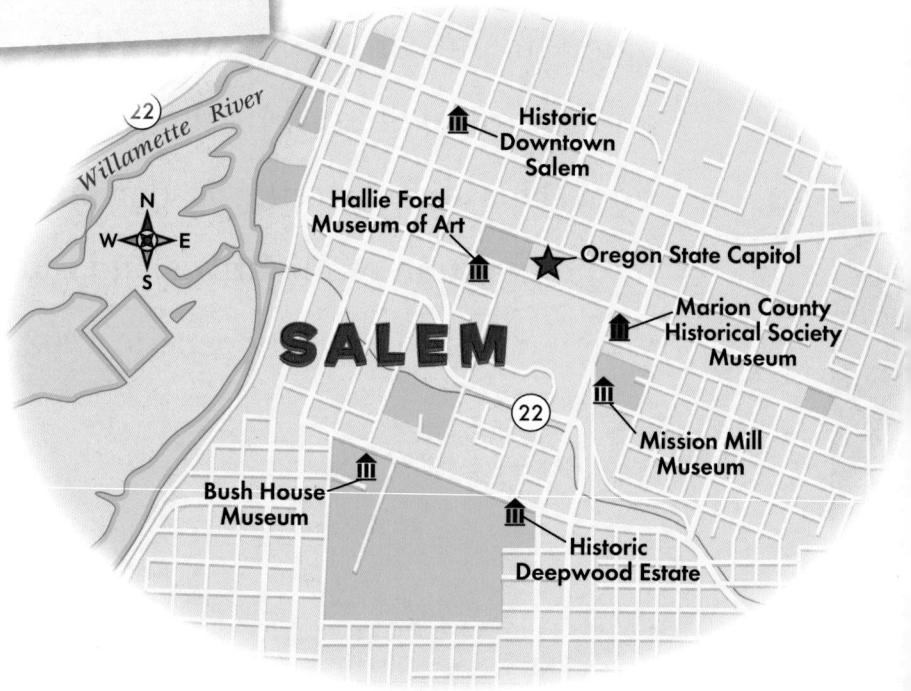

WOW

The pioneer statue on the Oregon state capitol is 23 feet (7 m) tall and weighs 8.5 tons!

Oregon State Government

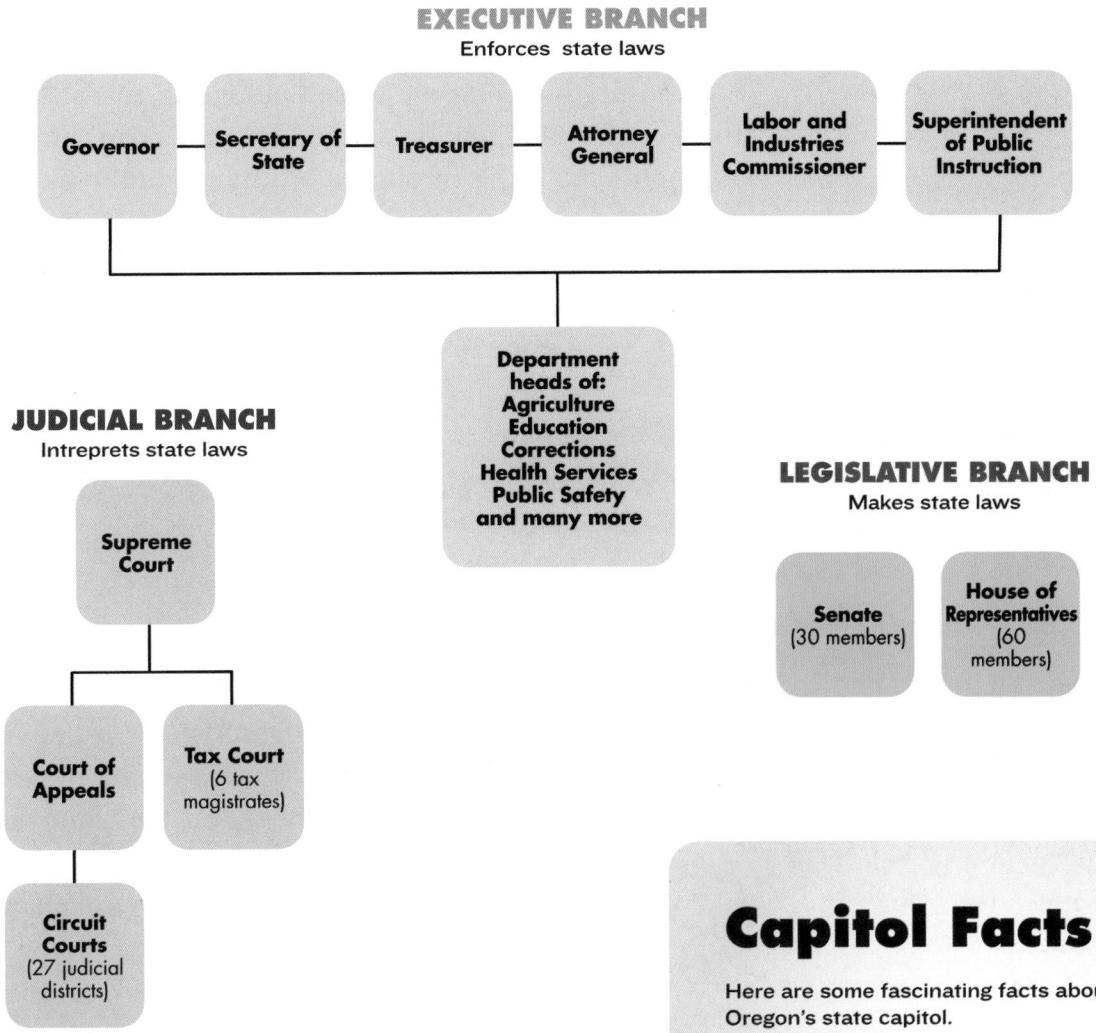

BRANCHES OF GOVERNMENT

Oregon's government is divided into three branches. The legislative branch makes the laws. The executive branch, or office of the governor, makes sure that the laws are followed. And the judicial branch, or court system, interprets the laws.

Capitol Facts

Here are some fascinating facts about Oregon's state capitol.

Height: 106 feet (32 m)
Opened: 1938
History: This is the third building to serve as the Oregon capitol. Fire destroyed the other two.
Interior: A bronze copy of the state seal is embedded in the floor.
Dome: Crowning the capitol's dome is a bronze statue of an Oregon pioneer covered with shiny gold leaf.

THE LEGISLATIVE BRANCH

Richard Chambers loved the outdoors. Yet wherever he went, he was dismayed to see empty cans and bottles that people thoughtlessly tossed along the roads. In the summer of 1968, Chambers urged his state representative to support recycling through a bill that would make disposable cans and bottles illegal in Oregon. In 1971, after much hard work by Chambers and many others, Oregon passed the Bottle Bill, requiring cans and bottles in the state to be returnable. Customers collect a deposit when they return bottles and cans to the store, and at the same time they help keep the state clean and beautiful. The Bottle Bill is just one example of how an Oregon citizen helped pass a law that makes life better for the state's people. The state led the nation with this initiative.

The legislature, officially called the Legislative Assembly, is divided into two houses, which meet in the four-story capitol. The upper house, or senate, has 30 members. State senators are elected to four-year terms. The lower house, or house of representatives, has 60 members who are elected to two-year terms. The assembly meets in odd-numbered years. Sessions begin on the second Monday in January and run until the assembly's work is done.

MINI-BIO

WAYNE MORSE: MAVERICK SENATOR

When he won a seat in the U.S. Senate in 1944, Oregon's Wayne Morse (1900–1974) ran as a Republican. In 1952, he left the Republican Party to become an Independent, then joined the Democrats in 1955. Morse's move earned him the nickname the Maverick Senator. (A maverick is a stray cow that wanders on the range.) Like a maverick of the West, he wasn't owned by anyone. He was often outspoken about government policies, including the Vietnam War. He served in the Senate until 1969.

Want to know more? Visit www.factsfornow.scholastic.com and enter the keyword **Oregon**.

THE EXECUTIVE BRANCH

A number of elected officials serve in Oregon's executive branch. They advise the governor and carry out specific tasks. These officials include the secretary of state, attorney general, treasurer, and superintendent of public instruction. Oregon's chief executive, the governor, is elected to a four-year term. Unlike many other states, Oregon does not have a lieutenant governor. If the governor cannot continue in office, the secretary of state takes over his or her duties.

The governor has many responsibilities, including creating a budget for the state government. He or she serves as commander of the state military and can call out forces to help in an emergency. The governor also signs bills into law or has the power to veto, or turn down, a bill. Each year, the governor delivers a speech called the State of the State address. In that speech, the governor outlines current conditions in the state and offers recommendations for improvements.

SEE IT HERE!

MAHONIA HALL

The official residence of Oregon's governor is a lovely mansion called Mahonia Hall. The state purchased Mahonia Hall in 1988. Built in 1924, Mahonia Hall has a magnificent third-floor ballroom and a built-in pipe organ.

MINI-BIO

MARK HATFIELD: SPEAKING HIS MIND

Mark Hatfield (1922–2011) was elected to the legislative assembly in 1950, and in 1956 became the youngest secretary of state in Oregon history. He served two terms as governor (1959–1967) before he stepped onto the national scene. He served in the U.S. Senate from 1967 to 1997. During the 1960s, he took a strong stand against the Vietnam War and called for a freeze on developing nuclear weapons. At the same time, he supported the farming and logging industries. Throughout his long career in politics, Hatfield never lost an election.

Want to know more? Visit www.factsfornow.scholastic.com and enter the keyword **Oregon**.

MINI-BIO

HERBERT HOOVER: OREGON'S PRESIDENT

Herbert Hoover (1874–1964) was born in Iowa but moved to Oregon to live with an uncle after his parents died. He lived in Newberg until 1891, when he entered Stanford University in California. During and after World War I, Hoover led the effort to feed the starving people of Europe. In 1928, he was elected president of the United States. He was in office when the Great Depression began, and many Americans harshly criticized him for failing to pull the country out of the crisis.

Want to know more? Visit www.factsfornow.scholastic.com and enter the keyword **Oregon**.

Representing Oregon

This list shows the number of elected officials who represent Oregon, both on the state and national levels.

OFFICE	NUMBER	LENGTH OF TERM
State senators	30	4 years
State representatives	60	2 years
U.S. senators	2	6 years
U.S. representatives	5	2 years
Presidential electors	7	—

THE JUDICIAL BRANCH

Oregon is divided into various circuit court districts. Judges in circuit courts rule on local civil cases, such as divorce and medical **malpractice**. They also handle criminal cases ranging from shoplifting to murder. Cases can be **appealed** from the circuit courts to the court of appeals and, finally, to the supreme court in Salem. The supreme court, the highest court in the state, has seven judges. Each judge is elected to serve a six-year term.

WORDS TO KNOW

malpractice *poor treatment that harms a patient*

appealed *asked a court to change the decision of a lower court*

LOCAL GOVERNMENT

Oregon has 36 counties and about 240 cities and towns. Towns and cities select their own form of government. Most small towns have a mayor and a town council. Most large cities have a form of government called council-manager. The city of Portland has an unusual form of government found nowhere else in the state. It is gov-

Oregon Counties

This map shows the 36 counties in Oregon. Salem, the state capital, is indicated with a star.

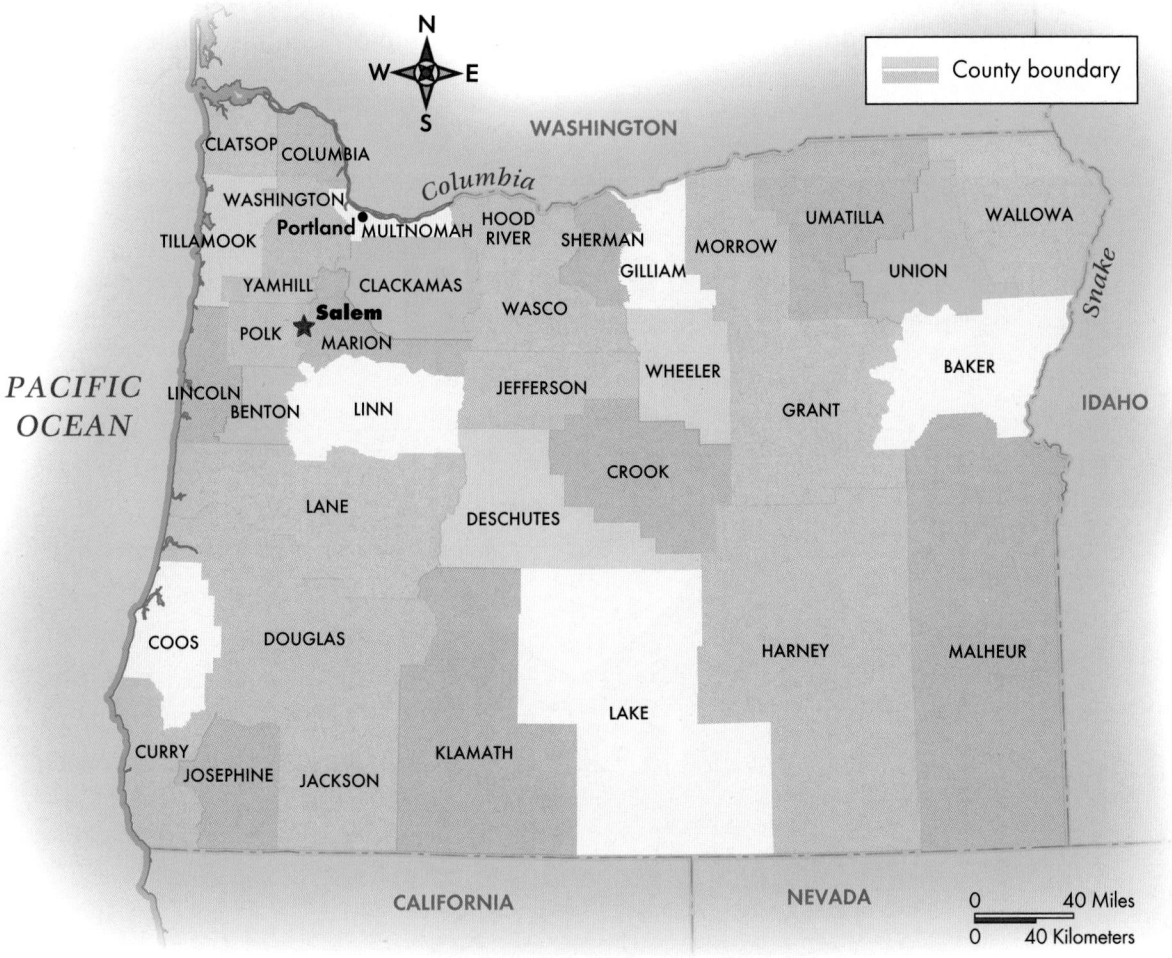

erned by a mayor and four officials called commissioners. These leaders help the mayor by managing various public programs.

State Flag

The state flag has a field of navy blue with the state seal in gold, which appears above the year in which Oregon became a state, 1859. The flag was officially adopted in 1925. The reverse side of the flag shows a beaver, the state animal. Oregon has the only state flag with an image on the back.

State Seal

The state seal is a shield with a bald eagle above it. Below the shield are 33 stars—signifying that Oregon was the 33rd state admitted to the Union—and a ribbon carrying the inscription "The Union." Above the ribbon are scenes that represent Oregon history. The mountains and forests of Oregon against the sun setting over the Pacific Ocean provide a background for an ox-drawn wagon, an elk, a departing British warship, and an arriving American merchant ship. Below the ribbon, a sheaf of wheat, a plow, and a miner's pick symbolize Oregon's resources and industries.

READ ABOUT

Doing Things for Others . . 100

Making Things 101

From Land and Sea 103

Workers harvest cranberries in Bandon.

ECONOMY

★

A FARMER DRIVES A TRACTOR OVER A FIELD NEAR PENDLETON. A chef prepares a meal in a health-food restaurant in Eugene. A clerk sells a pair of running shoes in a Beaverton store. In Portland, dockworkers load a containership bound for China. All of these people are contributing to Oregon's economy.

DOING THINGS FOR OTHERS

Service industries are industries in which people are paid to do things for others. A guide leading a group of mountain climbers up Mount Hood, a server in a Eugene restaurant delivering lunch to customers, and a Portland real estate agent taking a client to look at a new house all work in service industries. Service industries account for most of Oregon's **gross state product**. Finance, insurance, and real estate make up the largest segment of the state's service industries. Many of these industries are centered in the Portland area.

The service industries known as community, business, and personal services employ more people than any other segment of the economy. This group of service industries includes private lawyers and doctors, hairdressers, auto repair people, and electricians. Other important service industries include hospitality (restaurants and hotels) and wholesale and retail trade.

WORD TO KNOW

gross state product *the total value of all the goods and services produced in a state*

Construction workers are part of Oregon's service industry.

The state and federal governments employ thousands of service-industry workers in Oregon. Government employees include public school teachers, foresters, and workers in public hospitals. People who work at state colleges and universities are also government employees.

MAKING THINGS

Decades ago, people in Oregon relied on timber to keep the economy strong. But these days, business in Oregon is more focused on other industries.

In 1964, University of Oregon coach Bill Bowerman and a university track star named Phil Knight started a small company that sold shoes for athletes. The company expanded, and in 1971 it became Nike Footwear. Today, Nike, Inc., based in Beaverton, produces sportswear for people around the world. Nike is in keeping with Oregonians' tradition of athletic excellence and their love of the outdoors.

The high-technology industries are well established in Oregon. Two major computer manufacturers—Intel and Hewlett-Packard—have branches in the state.

Oregon's timber industry has given rise to the production of lumber and other wood-related products. Plants also turn out plywood, particleboard, and wood veneer. Machine shops in Oregon assemble equipment used in the wood-processing industries.

MINI-BIO

DOUGLAS ENGELBART: "FATHER OF THE INTERNET"

From the time he was a student at Oregon State University, Douglas Engelbart (1925–2013) dreamed of using technology to extend the reach of the human mind. He studied electrical engineering and quickly moved into the brand-new field of computer technology. In the 1960s, he pioneered a very early version of communication between computers using telephone lines. This online communication evolved into the Internet. Engelbart also invented a device for moving the cursor on a computer screen—the mouse.

Want to know more? Visit www.factsfornow.scholastic.com and enter the keyword **Oregon**.

SEE IT HERE!

A. C. GILBERT DISCOVERY VILLAGE

A. C. Gilbert of Salem believed that playing and learning went hand in hand. In 1911, he developed the idea for the Erector Set, a toy that has since taught millions of children about construction and engineering. You can explore many of Gilbert's more than 100 inventions at the A. C. Gilbert Discovery Village in Salem.

Major Agricultural and Mining Products

This map shows where Oregon's major agricultural and mining products come from. See a milk carton? That means dairy is found there.

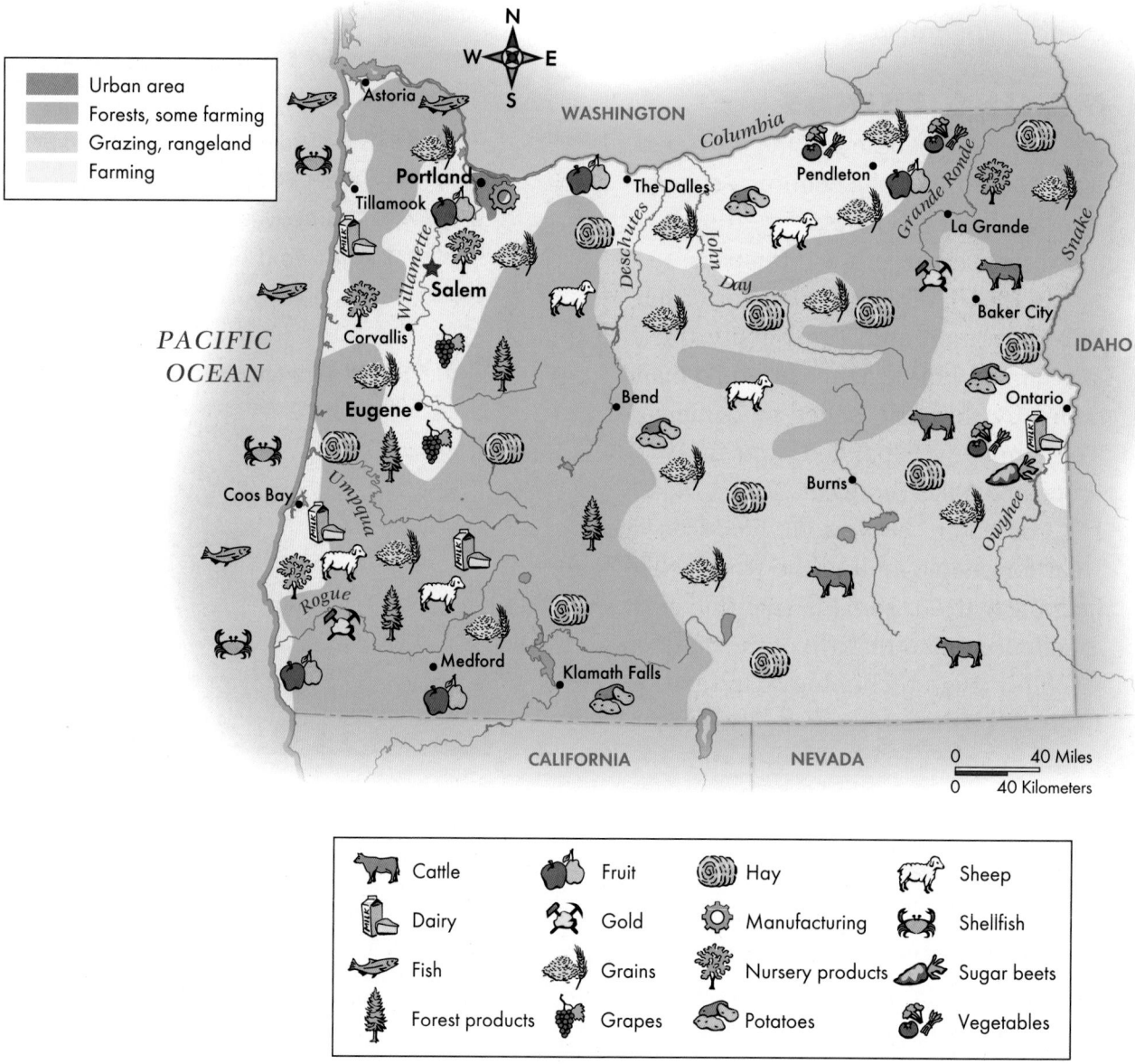

A cowgirl driving cattle near the Cascades

FROM LAND AND SEA

A good portion of Oregon's land is devoted to farming. Cattle and sheep graze on the high plateau east of the Cascades. Farmers in this region also grow wheat and potatoes. Western Oregon has many farms as well. The Willamette Valley is a leading producer of flowers and flower bulbs.

Top Products

Agriculture Bulbs and other nursery products, wheat, onions, potatoes, green peas, sweet corn, sugar beets, hazelnuts, timber, beef, wool

Manufacturing Electronic equipment, lumber and wood products, processed foods, fabricated metal products, paper products

Mining Sand and gravel, pumice, clay, lime

Fishing Albacore tuna, crabs, shrimp, whiting

A tulip farm in the Willamette Valley

Tulip, daffodil, narcissus, lily, and other bulbs from Oregon are shipped to gardeners all over the world.

Oregon is the nation's only major source of hazelnuts, or filberts. Tens of thousands of tons of hazelnuts are harvested from Oregon farms each year.

Nearly half of Oregon is covered with forests. Oregon is one of the nation's leading timber producers. Douglas fir, which grows west of the Cascades, is the state's chief timber export. Ponderosa pine, white fir, and lodgepole pine are logged in eastern Oregon.

WOW

Nearly all of the hazelnuts grown in the United States come from the Willamette Valley.

Sand and gravel for the construction industry are mined in most parts of Oregon. Oregon also contains deposits of clay, lime, and pumice. It is the only state to produce emery.

Fish was once the staple food in Oregon. Today, the fishing industry is still an important part of Oregon's economy. Crabs, shrimp, and salmon are harvested and sold commercially.

FAQ

Q8 WHAT IS EMERY?

A8 Emery is a black or dark gray mineral used for grinding and polishing. It is used in the manufacture of emery boards for filing fingernails and in the production of asphalt.

What Do Oregonians Do?

This color-coded chart shows what industries Oregonians work in.

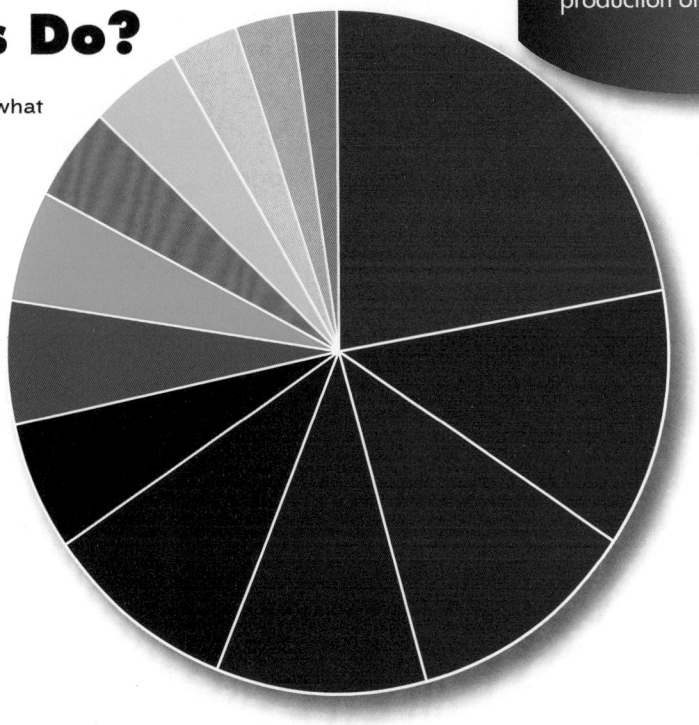

- **22.3%** Educational services, and health care and social assistance 388,867
- **12.3%** Retail trade 213,862
- **11.4%** Manufacturing 198,941
- **10.2%** Professional, scientific, and management, and administrative and waste management services 178,194
- **9.5%** Arts, entertainment, and recreation, and accommodation and food services 165,476
- **6.1%** Finance and insurance, and real estate and rental and leasing 105,708
- **5.9%** Construction 103,639
- **5.1%** Other services, except public administration 88,365
- **4.6%** Public administration 79,764
- **4.3%** Transportation and warehousing, and utilities 75,479
- **3.4%** Agriculture, forestry, fishing and hunting, and mining 59,519
- **2.9%** Wholesale trade 51,208
- **2.0%** Information 34,502

Source: U.S. Census Bureau, 2010 census

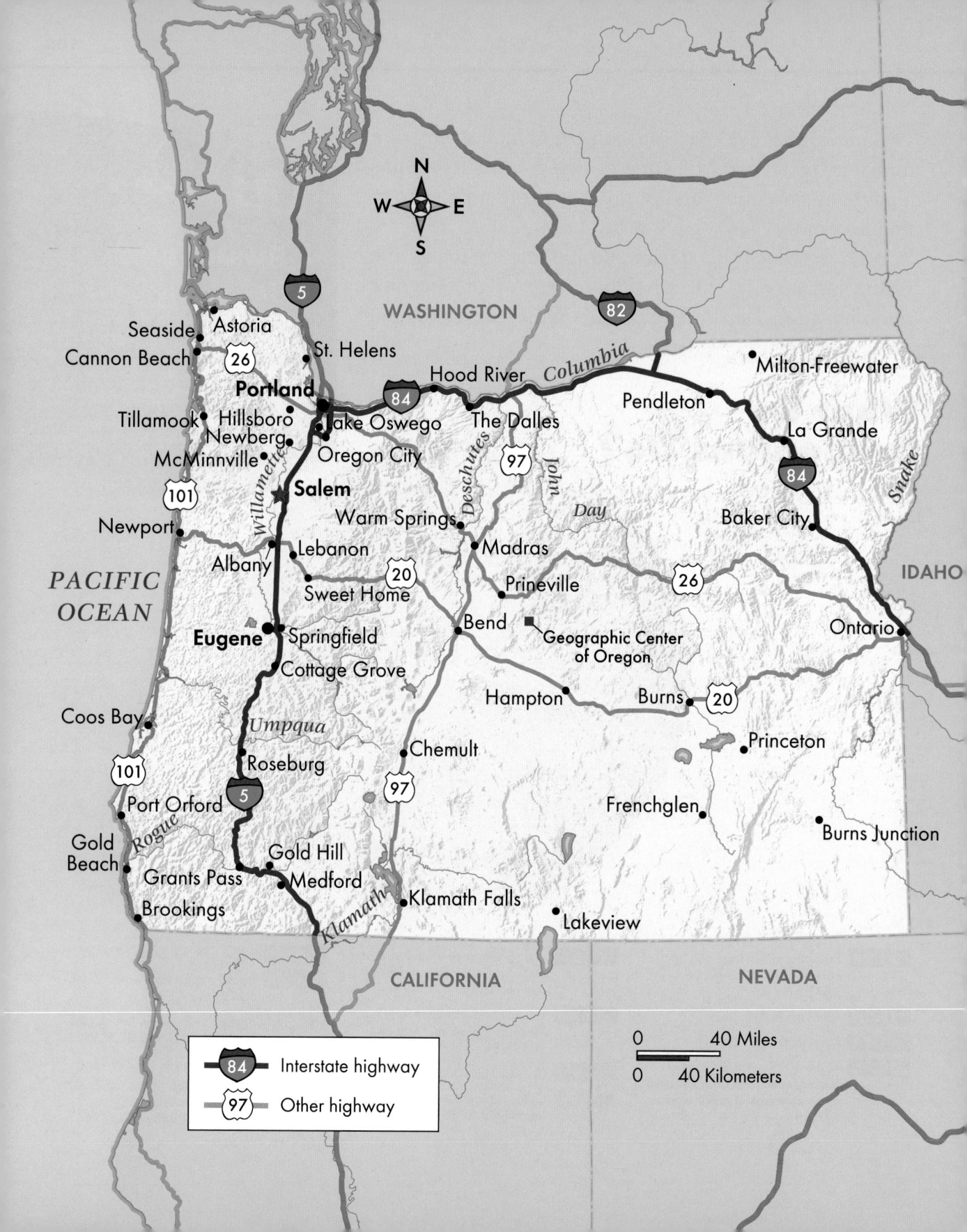
N
W
E
S
WASHINGTON
IDAHO
CALIFORNIA
NEVADA
PACIFIC OCEAN
Columbia
Snake
Willamette
Deschutes
John Day
Umpqua
Rogue
Klamath
Seaside
Astoria
Cannon Beach
St. Helens
Portland
Hillsboro
Tillamook
Newberg
Lake Oswego
Oregon City
McMinnville
Salem
Newport
Albany
Lebanon
Sweet Home
Eugene
Springfield
Cottage Grove
Coos Bay
Roseburg
Port Orford
Gold Beach
Gold Hill
Grants Pass
Medford
Brookings
Hood River
The Dalles
Warm Springs
Madras
Prineville
Bend
Geographic Center of Oregon
Chemult
Hampton
Burns
Klamath Falls
Lakeview
Frenchglen
Princeton
Burns Junction
Pendleton
Milton-Freewater
La Grande
Baker City
Ontario
5
82
84
26
101
97
20
0 40 Miles
0 40 Kilometers
Interstate highway
Other highway

TRAVEL GUIDE

★

FROM THE CRASHING WAVES OF THE PACIFIC COAST TO THE SNOW-CAPPED CASCADES, OREGON IS A LAND OF STUNNING NATURAL BEAUTY. Visit the state's beaches, hike its trails, observe its wildlife, and walk in the footsteps of people who lived long ago. And be sure to check out the museums listed on page 131 for even more cool stuff to see!

← Follow along with this map. We'll begin in Seaside and travel all the way to Ontario.

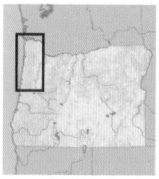

THE NORTHERN COAST

THINGS TO DO: Imagine camping with Lewis and Clark, taste local cheeses in Tillamook, or check out one of the world's tallest sea stacks.

Seaside

★ **Lewis and Clark Campsite:** Seaside is considered the official end of the Lewis and Clark Trail. The expedition's campsite has been reconstructed based on Clark's journals and sketches.

Cannon Beach

★ **Haystack Rock:** The tallest of Oregon's many sea stacks, Haystack Rock stands 235 feet (72 m) above the beach at low tide. Thousands of seabirds nest on it.

Haystack Rock

Astoria

★ **Fort Clatsop:** This was the winter encampment for the Corps of Discovery from December 1805 to March 1806. Visitors can tour the fort and an interpretive center—as well as hike some of the trails.

★ **Columbia River Maritime Museum:** View thousands of objects and photographs that tell the story of water travel and sea adventure in the Columbia River and the Pacific Northwest.

Tillamook

★ **Tillamook Cheese Visitor's Center:** Sample a variety of local cheeses at the edge of prime dairy country.

★ **Tillamook Forest Center:** This conservation center at the heart of the Tillamook Burn—an area ravaged by a series of wildfires in the 1930s and 1940s—tells the story of the natural disaster and how it changed forest management practices.

Haystack Rock is the third-tallest sea stack in the world!

Jellyfish at the Oregon Coast Aquarium

Newport

★ **Oregon Coast Aquarium:** See 190 species of birds, fish, and sea mammals at this aquarium, which sprawls over 29 acres (12 hectares). Seals, sea otters, and giant octopuses swim in their natural habitat. The aquarium includes the largest seabird **aviary** in North America.

★ **Yaquina Head Lighthouse:** Standing 93 feet (28 m) high, this lighthouse tower is the tallest on the Oregon coast. Climb to the top for a magnificent view of beaches, rocks, and waves.

Yaquina Head Lighthouse

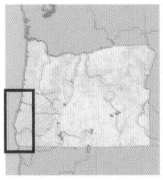

SOUTHERN COAST

THINGS TO DO: Watch towering waves at Shore Acres State Park, see fishing boats hoisted ashore at Port Orford, or explore Oregon's last working lighthouse.

Coos Bay

★ **Shore Acres State Park:** From a cliff-top shelter, look out to sea and watch for whales. Waves crash into the cliffs, sending jets of foam many feet into the air.

Port Orford

★ **Port Orford:** Each morning, the fishing boats are lowered into the water; each night, they are swung up and out on huge wooden booms. Why? This fishing center has no natural harbor.

Gold Beach

★ **Cape Blanco Lighthouse:** This familiar shore site is known as the last working lighthouse on Oregon's coast.

WORD TO KNOW

aviary *a large walk-in enclosure where birds are allowed to fly freely*

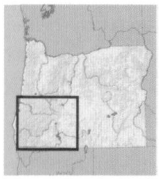

SOUTH-WESTERN OREGON

THINGS TO DO: Climb Lower Table Rock at Medford or challenge the force of gravity at the Oregon House of Mystery in Gold Hill.

Gold Hill

★ **Oregon House of Mystery:** Located in a strange area known as the Oregon Vortex, this museum challenges assumptions about gravity and perception. Balls seem to roll uphill, poles balance on end, and people appear to shrink or grow before your eyes.

Medford

★ **Lower Table Rock:** Take in a wonderful view of the Rogue River and the Siskiyou Mountains from the flat top of this giant rock. Upper Table Rock, nearby, is higher and easier to climb.

Lower Table Rock

The waterslide at Willamalane Park

WILLAMETTE VALLEY

THINGS TO DO: Glide down a giant waterslide, visit Herbert Hoover's boyhood home, or learn about the history of flight.

Springfield

★ **Willamalane Park and Recreation District:** This park features the only wave-action pool in the Northwest and a giant waterslide you won't forget!

Newberg

★ **Hoover-Minthorn House Museum:** Herbert Hoover, the 31st U.S. president, lived here with his aunt and uncle when he was a teenager. Many pieces of the family's furniture are on display. Young Herbert used to pick and eat pears from a tree that still grows and bears fruit on the grounds of the house.

McMinnville

★ **Evergeen Aviation & Space Museum:** This museum is home to the *Spruce Goose*, Howard Hughes's World War II "flying boat," and it features artifacts and information about the history of aviation.

The *Spruce Goose* at the Evergreen Aviation & Space Museum

Albany

★ **Monteith House:** Pioneers Walter and Thomas Monteith built this house in 1849. Over the years, the house served as a church, meeting-house, and military headquarters. It has been restored to look much as it did in the 1850s.

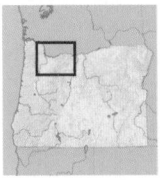

PORTLAND AREA

THINGS TO DO: Ride a trolley, stop and smell some roses, say hello to an elephant, or try on some hockey gear.

Lake Oswego

★ **Willamette Shore Trolley:** This train runs from Lake Oswego to Portland along the west bank of the Willamette River. The ride offers lovely river views, but be prepared to clatter through one of Oregon's darkest tunnels as well.

Portland

★ **Oregon Zoo:** The "wildest place in Oregon" features more than 2,000 animals, including many endangered species, and more than 1,000 species of exotic plants. Nearly 1.6 million people visit the zoo each year!

The rose garden at Washington Park

★ **Washington Park:** This lovely park in Portland's West Hills features a 5-acre (2 ha) Japanese garden that features flowers, shrubs, and cherry trees. The park zoo has many species of animals native to the Northwest, in addition to an exhibit of Asian elephants.

★ **Jamison Square:** During the warm summer months, visit this park to cool off. Play in the shallow fountain located here, take a look at the sculptures that decorate the square, or just sit back on the steps and people watch. The fountain is also open during the spring and autumn.

★ **Oregon Historical Society:** The society's museum features exhibits about Oregon art, World War II, and other aspects of the state's history.

★ **International Rose Test Garden:** Portland is sometimes called the Rose City, and this magnificent park helps explain why. In spring and summer, it is alive with color and fragrance as some 400 varieties of roses burst into bloom.

★ **Oregon Museum of Science and Industry:** Visitors will find five exhibit halls, eight science labs, a big-screen Empirical Theater, and a planetarium. Learn about science by touching a volcano, experiencing an earthquake, or uncovering a fossil!

Innovation Station at the Oregon Museum of Science and Industry

MINI-BIO

HENRY LEWIS PITTOCK: THE MAN BEHIND THE *OREGONIAN*

When he was 17, Henry Lewis Pittock (1836–1919) left Pittsburgh and set out for Oregon. According to some stories, he made the entire journey barefoot! He arrived nearly penniless and took a job as a printer with a weekly paper called the *Weekly Oregonian*. At first, room and board were his only wages. Pittock was a hard worker and clever businessman, and he took over the paper when the owner left in 1860. He built what became the *Morning Oregonian* into the state's leading daily newspaper. He also established a thriving paper mill, which spurred Oregon's papermaking industry.

Want to know more? Visit www.factsfornow.scholastic.com and enter the keyword **Oregon**.

★ **Pittock Mansion:** Completed in 1912 by publisher Henry Pittock, this mansion has 22 rooms that have been restored to look as they did early in the 20th century. From the grounds, you can see a breathtaking view of downtown Portland and the mountains to the east.

Oregon City

★ **McLoughlin House:** Although it has been moved from its original location, this house looks much as it did when Dr. John McLoughlin lived here in 1846. Furniture, paintings, and documents tell the story of the man remembered as the Father of Oregon.

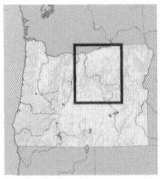

NORTH CENTRAL OREGON

THINGS TO DO: Discover the culture of the high desert or admire Mount Hood from a railcar.

Bend

★ **High Desert Museum:** This facility celebrates the wildlife, culture, art, and natural resources of the High Desert region.

The Dalles

★ **Columbia Gorge Discovery Center:** Exhibits reveal the geology, plants, animals, artifacts, and history of the Columbia River Gorge and Wasco County.

★ **Sorosis Park:** This 15-acre (6 ha) park on the cliffs offers a splendid view of the city and the Columbia River Gorge. Missionaries once preached from the park's Sermon Rock.

Hood River

★ **Mount Hood Railroad:** A ride on the scenic railroad is a wonderful way to enjoy spectacular views of Mount Hood and the Columbia River Gorge. The train is pulled by a classic diesel engine.

Warm Springs

★ **Museum at Warm Springs:** Located on the Warm Springs Indian Reservation, this museum offers exhibits and educational programs about Native American heritage. See how early peoples lived and what clothing they wore.

Mount Hood Railroad

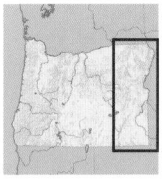

EASTERN OREGON

THINGS TO DO: Wander through a gold-rush ghost town, learn about the Oregon Trail from a unique perspective, or hike Steens Mountain for a spectacular view.

Baker City

★ **Auburn ghost town:** On October 23, 1863, a prospector named Henry Griffin discovered gold in Auburn, and in six months it became a booming gold-rush town of 6,000 people. The gold didn't last, and by 1867 Auburn was a ghost town. Wander through the crumbled remains of houses and stores, and try to imagine the eager miners who once made Auburn their home.

Boardman

★ **SAGE Center:** Opened in 2013, this visitor center focuses on agriculture and energy in the region. Find out how potatoes are turned into french fries, learn where in the world local products are shipped, and take part in a number of interactive exhibits.

La Grande

★ **Ladd Marsh Wildlife Area:** This once-threatened wetland has been carefully restored and is now alive with herons, ducks, and other waterfowl. Bring your wading boots and binoculars, and see how many species you can spot!

Pendleton

★ **Tamástslikt Cultural Institute:** The institute presents the history and achievements of the Cayuses, Walla Wallas, and Umatillas of eastern Oregon. The story of the Indians is told in three sections: "We Were," "We Are," and "We Will Be." Find out what Native Americans thought about the Oregon Trail.

An exhibit at the Tamástslikt Cultural Institute

Steens Mountain

Frenchglen

★ **Steens Mountain:** This mountain has a variety of trails for both beginning and more experienced climbers to enjoy. The view from the peak is well worth the effort!

Ontario

★ **Four Rivers Cultural Center:** This museum traces the many cultures that have merged in Oregon's Treasure Valley. Displays tell the stories of the Northern Paiutes, Japanese Americans, Latinos, and European Americans who made the region their home.

WRITING PROJECTS

Check out these ideas for creating campaign brochures and writing you-are-there editorials. Or research famous Oregonians.

118

ART PROJECTS

Create a great PowerPoint presentation, illustrate the state song, or learn about the state quarter and design your own.

119

TIMELINE

What happened when? This timeline highlights important events in the state's history—and shows what was happening throughout the United States at the same time.

122

GLOSSARY

Remember the Words to Know from the chapters in this book? They're all collected here.

125

FAST FACTS

Use this section to find fascinating facts about state symbols, land area and population statistics, weather, sports teams, and much more.

126

SCIENCE, TECHNOLOGY, ENGINEERING, & MATH PROJECTS 120

Make weather maps, graph population statistics, and research endangered species that live in the state.

PRIMARY VS. SECONDARY SOURCES 121

So what are primary and secondary sources? And what's the diff? This section explains all that and where you can find them.

BIOGRAPHICAL DICTIONARY 133

This at-a-glance guide highlights some of the state's most important and influential people. Visit this section and read about their contributions to the state, the country, and the world.

RESOURCES 138

Books and much more. Take a look at these additional sources for information about the state.

WRITING PROJECTS

Write a Memoir, Journal, or Editorial for Your School Newspaper!

Picture Yourself . . .

★ fishing the rivers along Oregon's coast in the 1790s. Where would you fish, and what tools would you use? How would you dry and store the fish you catch?

SEE: Chapter Two, pages 24–28.

★ on the Oregon Trail. You are with your family, traveling hundreds of miles with no end in sight. What would your responsibilities be?

SEE: Chapter Three, pages 44–46.

Create an Election Brochure or Web Site!

Run for office! Throughout this book, you've read about some issues that concern Oregon today. As a candidate for governor of Oregon, create a campaign brochure or Web site.

★ Explain how you meet the qualifications to be governor of Oregon.

★ Talk about the three or four major issues you'll focus on if you're elected.

★ Remember, you'll be responsible for Oregon's budget. How would you spend the taxpayers' money?

SEE: Chapter Seven, pages 91–94.

Create an Interview Script with a Person from Oregon!

★ Research various Oregonians, such as Mel Blanc, Beverly Cleary, Matt Groening, Mary Decker Slaney, or Phil Knight.

★ Based on your research, pick one person you would most like to talk with.

★ Write a script of the interview. What questions would you ask? How would this person answer? Create a question-and-answer format. You may want to supplement this writing project with a voice-recording dramatization of the interview.

SEE: Chapters Five, Six, and Seven, pages 62–95, and the Biographical Dictionary, pages 133–137.

Nike CEO Phil Knight

ART PROJECTS

Create a PowerPoint Presentation or Visitors' Guide

Welcome to Oregon!

Oregon's a great place to visit and to live! From its natural beauty to its bustling cities and historical sites, there's plenty to see and do. In your PowerPoint presentation or brochure, highlight 10 to 15 of Oregon's amazing landmarks. Be sure to include:

★ a map of the state showing where these sites are located

★ photos, illustrations, Web links, natural history facts, geographic stats, climate and weather, plants and wildlife, and recent discoveries

SEE: Chapter Nine, pages 106–115, and Fast Facts, pages 126–127.

Illustrate the Lyrics to the Oregon State Song

("Oregon, My Oregon")

Use markers, paints, photos, collages, colored pencils, or computer graphics to illustrate the lyrics to "Oregon, My Oregon." Turn your illustrations into a picture book, or scan them into PowerPoint and add music.

SEE: The lyrics to "Oregon, My Oregon" on page 128.

Research Oregon's State Quarter

From 1999 to 2008, the U.S. Mint introduced new quarters commemorating each of the 50 states in the order that they were admitted to the Union. Each state's quarter features a unique design on its reverse, or back.

Research and write an essay explaining:

★ Research the significance of the image. Who designed the quarter? Who chose the final design?

★ Design your own Oregon quarter. What images would you choose for the reverse?

★ Make a poster showing the Oregon quarter and label each image.

GO TO: www.factsfornow.scholastic.com. Enter the keyword **Oregon** and look for the link to the Oregon quarter.

SCIENCE, TECHNOLOGY, ENGINEERING, & MATH PROJECTS

Graph Population Statistics!

★ Compare population statistics (such as ethnic background, birth, death, and literacy rates) in Oregon counties or major cities.

★ On your graph or chart, look at population density and write sentences describing what the population statistics show; graph one set of population statistics and write a paragraph explaining what the graphs reveal.

SEE: Chapter Six, pages 76–77.

Create a Weather Map of Oregon!

Use your knowledge of Oregon's geography to research and identify conditions that result in specific weather events. What is it about the geography of Oregon that makes it vulnerable to things such as thunderstorms and heavy rainfall? Create a weather map or poster that shows the weather patterns across the state. Include a caption explaining the technology used to measure weather phenomena and provide data.

SEE: Chapter One, pages 8–16.

Northern spotted owl

Track Endangered Species

Using your knowledge of Oregon's wildlife, research which animals and plants are endangered or threatened.

★ Find out what the state is doing to protect these species.

★ Chart known populations of the animals and plants, and report on changes in certain geographic areas.

SEE: Chapter One, pages 17–21.

PRIMARY VS. SECONDARY SOURCES

What's the Diff?

Your teacher may require at least one or two primary sources and one or two secondary sources for your assignment. So, what's the difference between the two?

★ **Primary sources are original.** You are reading the actual words of someone's diary, journal, letter, autobiography, or interview. Primary sources can also be photographs, maps, prints, cartoons, news/film footage, posters, first-person newspaper articles, drawings, musical scores, and recordings. By the way, when you conduct a survey, interview someone, shoot a video, or take photographs to include in a project, you are creating primary sources!

★ **Secondary sources are what you find in encyclopedias, textbooks, articles, biographies, and almanacs.** These are written by a person or group of people who tell about something that happened to someone else. Secondary sources also recount what another person said or did. This book is an example of a secondary source.

Now that you know what primary sources are—where can you find them?

★ **Your school or local library:** Check the library catalog for collections of original writings, government documents, musical scores, and so on. Some of this material may be stored on microfilm.

★ **Historical societies:** These organizations keep historical documents, photographs, and other materials.
Staff members can help you find what you are looking for. History museums are also great places to see primary sources firsthand.

★ **The Internet:** There are lots of sites that have primary sources you can download and use in a project or assignment.

TIMELINE

★ ★ ★

U.S. Events

1565
Spanish admiral Pedro Menéndez de Avilés founds St. Augustine, Florida, the oldest continuously occupied European settlement in the continental United States.

1607
The first permanent English settlement in North America is established at Jamestown.

1619
The first African indentured laborers in English North America are purchased for work in the Jamestown settlement.

1620
Pilgrims found Plymouth Colony, the second permanent English settlement.

1682
René-Robert Cavelier, Sieur de La Salle, claims more than 1 million square miles (2.6 million sq km) of territory in the Mississippi River basin for France, naming it Louisiana.

1754–63
England and France fight over North American colonial lands in the French and Indian War. By the end of the war, France has ceded all of its land west of the Mississippi to Spain and its Canadian territories to England.

1500

Oregon Events

1543
A Spanish ship sails up the Pacific coast to what is now southern Oregon.

1577
Sir Francis Drake sails to the coast of Oregon and claims the land for England.

1600

A Nez Perce man on horseback

1700

1720s
Horses reach the Columbia Plateau and change life for the Native people there.

U.S. Events

1776
Thirteen American colonies declare their independence from Great Britain.

1787
The U.S. Constitution is written.

1803
The Louisiana Purchase almost doubles the size of the United States.

1812–15
The United States and Great Britain fight the War of 1812.

1830
The Indian Removal Act forces eastern Native American groups to relocate west of the Mississippi River.

1846–48
The United States fights a war with Mexico over western territories in the Mexican War.

1861–65
The American Civil War is fought between the Northern Union and the Southern Confederacy; it ends with the surrender of the Confederate army, led by General Robert E. Lee.

1800

Oregon Events

Robert Gray

1792
Captain Robert Gray becomes the first American to see the mouth of the Columbia River.

1805–06
Lewis and Clark spend the winter at Fort Clatsop near the mouth of the Columbia.

1834
Jason Lee establishes a mission in the Willamette Valley.

1840s
Thousands of Americans travel to Oregon along the Oregon Trail.

1848
Oregon becomes a U.S. territory.

1851
Gold is found in southern Oregon.

1859
Oregon becomes the 33rd state in the Union.

U.S. Events

1898
The United States gains control of Puerto Rico, the Philippines, and Guam after defeating Spain in the Spanish-American War.

1900

1917–18
The United States engages in World War I.

1929
The stock market crashes, plunging the United States more deeply into the Great Depression.

1941–45
The United States engages in World War II.

1950–53
The United States engages in the Korean War.

1964–73
The United States engages in the Vietnam War.

2000

2001
Terrorists hijack four U.S. aircraft and crash them into the World Trade Center in New York City, the Pentagon in Arlington, Virginia, and a Pennsylvania field, killing thousands.

2003
The United States and coalition forces invade Iraq.

Oregon Events

1877
The Wallowa band of Nez Perces refuses to move to a reservation and leads the U.S. Army on a four-month chase.

Nez Perce War

1902
The Oregon constitution is changed to allow voters to place initiatives and referendums on the ballot.

1912
Oregon women gain the right to vote.

1938
The Bonneville Lock and Dam is completed on the Columbia River.

1942
Japanese Americans are sent to internment camps during World War II.

1971
Oregon passes the "Bottle Bill" to help clean up the environment.

2014
Oregon's state minimum wage is raised to $9.10 an hour.

GLOSSARY

amendment a change to a law or legal document

appealed asked a court to change the decision of a lower court

archaeologists people who study the remains of past human societies

aviary a large walk-in enclosure where birds are allowed to fly freely

breechcloths garments worn by men over their lower bodies

emigrants people who leave their homes to live in another land

glaciers slow-moving masses of ice

gross state product the total value of all the goods and services produced in a state

hydroelectric power electricity generated by the force of water passing over a dam

immunity natural protection against disease

internment camps places where people are confined, usually during wartime

malpractice poor treatment that harms a patient

missionaries people who try to convert others to a religion

missions places created by a religious group to spread its beliefs

obsidian jet-black volcanic glass

pemmican dried meat that was sometimes mixed with dried berries

plateau an elevated part of the earth with steep slopes

quadriplegic totally or partially paralyzed from the neck down

recall to remove elected officials from office

reservations lands set aside for Native Americans to live on

segregated separated from others according to race, class, ethnic group, religion, or other factors

suffrage the right to vote

symmetry balance, evenness on both sides

taboos rules about how activities such as hunting and preparing food must be performed

transcontinental crossing an entire continent

tributary a river that flows into a larger river

FAST FACTS

State Symbols

State seal

Statehood date February 14, 1859, 33rd state
Origin of state name Unknown, but one theory holds that the name may have come from the French word *ouragan*, meaning "hurricane"
State capital Salem
State nickname The Beaver State
State motto "She flies with her own wings"
State bird Western meadowlark
State flower Oregon grape
State fish Chinook salmon
State mammal Beaver
State insect Oregon swallowtail
State nut Hazelnut
State song "Oregon, My Oregon"
State tree Douglas fir
State shell Oregon hairy triton
State gemstone Oregon sunstone
State rock Thunderegg
State fair Late August–early September at Salem

Geography

Total area; rank 98,379 square miles (254,801 sq km); 9th
Land; rank 95,985 square miles (248,601 sq km); 10th
Water; rank 2,394 square miles (6,200 sq km); 20th
Inland water; rank 1,063 square miles (2,753 sq km); 21st
Geographic center Crook, 25 miles (40 km) south-southeast of Prineville
Latitude 42° N to 46°15′ N
Longitude 116°45′ W to 124°30′ W
Highest point Mount Hood, 11,239 feet (3,426 m)
Lowest point Sea level along the Pacific Ocean
Largest city Portland
Number of counties 36

Population

Population; rank (2010 census)	3,831,074; 27th
Density (2010 census)	40 persons per square mile (15 per sq km)
Population distribution (2010 census)	81% urban, 19% rural
Ethnic distribution (2010 census)	White persons: 78.5% Persons of Hispanic or Latino origin: 11.7% Asian persons: 3.6% Persons reporting two or more races: 2.9% Black persons: 1.7% American Indian and Alaska Native persons: 1.1% Native Hawaiian and other Pacific Islanders: 0.3% Persons of some other race: 0.1%

Weather

Record high temperature	119°F (48°C) at Prineville on July 29, 1898, and at Pendleton on August 10, 1898
Record low temperature	–54°F (–48°C) at Ukiah on February 9, 1933, and at Seneca on February 10, 1933
Average July temperature, Portland	68°F (20°C)
Average January temperature, Portland	41°F (5°C)
Average annual precipitation, Portland	36 inches (91 cm)

State flag

STATE SONG

"Oregon, My Oregon"

In 1920, a competition was held to select a state song for Oregon. The words to the winning song, "Oregon, My Oregon," were written by J. A. Buchanan, and the music is by Henry B. Murtagh. It was adopted as the state song in 1927.

Land of the empire builders, land of the golden west;
Conquered and held by free men, fairest and the best.
Onward and upward ever, forward and on and on;
Hail to thee, land of heroes, my Oregon.

Land of the rose and sunshine, land of the summer's breeze;
Laden with health and vigor, fresh from Western seas.
Blest by the blood of martyrs, land of the setting sun;
Hail to thee, land of Promise; my Oregon.

NATURAL AREAS AND HISTORIC SITES

National Park

Crater Lake National Park sits on the site of a volcano that erupted and collapsed almost 7,000 years ago. Crater Lake lies inside the collapsed volcano. Most of the year, the park is covered in snow, so snowshoers and cross-country skiers abound. In the summer, visitors can drive around the rim of the lake, hike the many trails, take boat tours, scuba dive, and fish.

National Monuments

The *Oregon Caves National Monument* features deep limestone caverns filled with stalactites, stalagmites, stone shelves and benches, and crystal clear pools.

The *Newberry National Volcanic Monument* includes 50,000 acres (20,234 ha) of lakes, lava flows, and volcanic mountains.

National Historical Parks

Lewis and Clark National Historical Park features the sites where Lewis and Clark first saw the Pacific Ocean and prepared for their return trip home.

The *Nez Perce National Historical Park* commemorates the stories and history of the Native Americans. The 38 sites of this park are found in Idaho, Oregon, Washington, and Montana.

National Memorial

Lewis and Clark and their Corps of Discovery spent the winter of 1805–1806 in a roughly built wooden fort near present-day *Fort Clatsop National Memorial*. The original fort is gone, but in 1955, Oregon citizens built a replica, using Clark's sketches.

National Historic Trails

Oregon has three different national historic trails, each with its own unique historical significance. They are the *California National Historic Trail*, the *Lewis and Clark National Historic Trail*, and the *Oregon National Historic Trail*.

National Recreation Area

Over thousands of years, the wind has swept sand into fantastic sculpted mounds at *Oregon Dunes National Recreation Area*, which visitors can explore on foot or by camel.

National Forests

Oregon has 11 national forests scattered throughout the state. Southwest Oregon's *Siskiyou National Forest*, part of the Siskiyou Mountain Range extending into northern California, has the most diverse ecology in the Pacific Northwest. *Umatilla National Forest* in northeast Oregon is located in the Blue Mountains.

SPORTS TEAMS

★ ★ ★

NCAA Teams (Division I)

Oregon State University *Beavers*
Portland State University *Vikings*
University of Oregon *Ducks*
University of Portland *Pilots*

PROFESSIONAL SPORTS TEAMS

★ ★ ★

National Basketball Association

Portland *Trail Blazers*

Major League Soccer

Portland *Timbers*

CULTURAL INSTITUTIONS

Libraries

The *Oregon Historical Society Library* in Portland has existed for more than 100 years. Its collections include pioneer memorabilia, Native American artwork, and various other historical collections.

The *Oregon Collection at the University of Oregon* (Eugene) contains materials about the history, literature, and life in Oregon and Oregon Territory. A microfilm collection includes the largest collection of Oregon newspapers in the world.

The *Oregon State Archives* (Salem) is part of the Office of the Oregon Secretary of State. The collection features maps, photographs, county histories, biographies of notable Oregonians, and other historical material.

Museums

The *Columbia River Maritime Museum* celebrates Astoria's tradition as a port city.

The *University of Oregon Museum of Natural and Cultural History* (Eugene) houses traditional fabrics, tools, weapons, and art from Africa, Asia, and New Guinea, as well as the Pacific Northwest.

The *Oregon Museum of Science and Industry* (Portland) has more than 200 hands-on exhibits.

The *Portland Art Museum* has distinguished collections of Asian, European, and Native American art, as well as works by Oregon and Washington artists.

The *Chinese House Railroad Museum* (Echo) offers a glimpse of the railroad-building era, including a reconstructed bunkhouse where Chinese laborers lived.

The *Favell Museum* (Klamath Falls) preserves the art and tools of Oregon's Native peoples.

Performing Arts

The *Oregon Symphony* (Portland) performs classical compositions, popular and gospel music, jazz, and much more.

The *Portland Opera* showcases classical international operas, modern works, and Broadway musicals, comedies, and dramas.

Universities and Colleges

In 2011, Oregon had 9 public and 29 private institutions of higher learning.

ANNUAL EVENTS

January–March

Sled Dog Races in Chemult (January–February)

Seafood and Wine Festival in Newport (late February)

April–June

Pear Blossom Festival in Medford (mid-April)

All Northwest Barbershop Ballad Contest and Gay Nineties Festival in Forest Grove (early May)

All-Indian Rodeo in Tygh Valley (mid-May)

Rhododendron Festival in Florence (mid-May)

Cannon Beach Sandcastle Contest in Cannon Beach (May)

Fleet of Flowers Memorial Service in Depoe Bay (late May)

Oregon Shakespeare Festival in Ashland (May through October)

Strawberry Festival in Lebanon (early June)

Rose Festival and parade in Portland (June)

Bach Summer Music Festival in Eugene (late June)

July–September

Buckeroo in Molalla (early July)

Butte to Butte 10K in Eugene (early July)

Port Orford Jubilee Celebration (Fourth of July)

Rodeo in St. Paul (early July)

World Class Windsurfing in Hood River (July)

Chief Joseph Days in Joseph (late July)

Oregon Brewers Festival in Portland (late July)

Regatta in Astoria (mid-August)

State Fair in Salem (August–September)

Cycle Oregon Bike Ride in different locations (September)

Pendleton Round-Up (September)

Oktoberfest in Mount Angel (mid-September)

October–December

Lord's Acre Auction and Barbecue in Powell Butte (early November)

Kraut and Sausage Feed and Bazaar in Verboort (November)

Whale-Watching on the Oregon coast (November–December)

BIOGRAPHICAL DICTIONARY

Goli Ameri

Danny Ainge (1959–) is a Eugene-born basketball player. He played with the Boston Celtics, Portland Trail Blazers, and Phoenix Suns.

Goli Ameri (1956–), who was born in Iran and later moved to Oregon, is a diplomat and businessperson. She is currently president of the Center for Global Engagement, an organization devoted to promoting peace among world nations. She is a former assistant secretary of state and U.S. delegate to the United Nations.

John Jacob Astor (1763–1848) was an investor who organized the Pacific Fur Company in 1810 and established Astoria in 1812.

Walter Backman (1959–) is a Hillboro-born baseball player who played in the Major Leagues from 1980 to 1993. He was a member of the 1986 New York Mets World Series champion team.

Frederic Homer Balch (1861–1891), born in Lebanon, was a writer best known for his novel *The Bridge of the Gods*.

James Beard (1903–1985) was a chef and food writer, best known for bringing French cuisine to Americans in the 1950s with his television cooking show, the first in the United States. He was born and grew up in Portland.

Pietro Belluschi See page 80.

Don Berry (1931–2001) wrote novels about life on the Oregon frontier. He was born in Minnesota and moved to Oregon as a young man.

Mel Blanc (1908–1989) was the voice behind cartoon characters such as Bugs Bunny, Porky Pig, and Barney Rubble of *The Flintstones*. He grew up in Portland.

Benjamin Louis Eulalie de Bonneville (1796–1878) was a soldier who arrived in Oregon in 1832 as part of a three-year exploration of the West. He mapped much of the West and blazed part of the Oregon Trail.

Bill Bowerman (1911–1999) was a track coach at the University of Oregon who led his team to 16 winning seasons and coached many outstanding runners. He cofounded Nike, Inc.

John Callahan (1951–2010) was a Portland cartoonist and writer. He was paralyzed in a car accident, and his work often found humor in disabilities and other difficulties.

Beatrice Morrow Cannady See page 71.

Beatrice Morrow Cannady

Raymond Carver (1938–1988) wrote intense stories, usually about working-class people. His collections include *Cathedral* and *Where I'm Calling From*. He was born in Clatskanie.

Marilyn Chin (1955–) is a Hong Kong–born poet who grew up in Portland. Many of her poems explore and celebrate the Asian American experience.

Beverly Cleary See page 81.

Pinto Colvig (1892–1967), born in Jacksonville, was an actor and circus performer best known as the original Bozo the Clown and the first voice of Walt Disney's Goofy.

Concomly (1760?–?) was a Chinook leader who helped the Lewis and Clark expedition and the founders of Astoria.

Ann Curry (1956–) is a TV journalist who grew up in Ashland and graduated from the University of Oregon.

Harold Lenoir (H. L.) Davis (1894–1960), born in Nonpareil, wrote stories of frontier life in the northwestern United States. He won the 1936 Pulitzer Prize for *Honey in the Horn*.

Ann Curry

Jacoby Ellsbury

Roscoe Lee Dixon See page 58.

David Douglas (1799–1834) was a Scottish-born botanist who explored Oregon in 1824–1825. The Douglas fir is named in his honor.

Abigail Scott Duniway See page 66.

Jacoby Ellsbury (1983–) is a professional baseball player who was born in Madras. He is the first person of Navajo descent to play in major league baseball.

Douglas Engelbart See page 101.

Alfred Carlton (A. C.) Gilbert (1884–1961) was a toymaker and businessman best known as the inventor of the Erector Set, a metal construction set, introduced in 1913. He was born in Salem.

Robert Gray (1755–1806) was a fur trader and explorer who became the first American sea captain to see the mouth of the Columbia River. He named the river after his ship.

Edith Starrett Green See page 90.

Matt Groening (1954–) is a cartoonist who created *The Simpsons*. He was born in Portland.

Moses Harris (?–?) was an African American trapper and guide who led wagon trains along the Oregon Trail.

Mark Hatfield See page 93.

Ernest Haycox See page 83.

Herbert Hoover See page 94.

Joni Huntley (1956–) won the bronze medal in the women's high jump at the 1984 Summer Olympics in Los Angeles. In 1975, she won a gold medal in the same event at the Pan American Games in Mexico. She was born in McMinnville.

Lawson Fusao Inada (1938–) is a poet who writes about the experience and culture of Japanese Americans. He was chosen as Oregon's poet laureate in 2006.

Terri Irwin (1964–) is a naturalist who was born in Eugene. She is the widow of naturalist Steve Irwin and currently lives in Australia, where she owns the Australia Zoo.

Terri Irwin

Ken Kesey

Luther Jerstad (1937–1998) was among the first Americans to reach the summit of Mount Everest, in 1963. He lived in Portland.

Chief Joseph (1840–1904), born in Wallowa Valley, was a leader of the local band of Nez Perce Native Americans. He and his followers fought many battles against the U.S. Army in the Northwest, before surrendering in 1877. He was known to the Nez Perces as Hinmuuttu-yalatlat (Thunder Rolling Down Mountain).

Miranda July (1974–), born Miranda Jennifer Grossinger, is a filmmaker and short-story writer who lived in Portland for many years.

Ken Kesey (1935–2001) was a novelist who grew up in Springfield. He set his novels *One Flew over the Cuckoo's Nest* and *Sometimes a Great Notion* in Oregon.

Phil Knight (1938–), born and raised in Portland, is the cofounder of the Nike sports footwear and clothing company. He made his first sales out of the back of his car at track meets across the Northwest.

Jon Krakauer (1954–) of Corvallis writes about the outdoors. His best-selling *Into Thin Air* (1997) tells the story of a disastrous trek up Mount Everest, the world's highest peak.

Joseph Lane (1801–1881) was a soldier and politician who served as the first governor of the Oregon Territory (1849–1850).

Jason Lee (1803–1845) was a missionary who came to the Oregon Country in 1834 and established several missions among the Indians. In 1842, he founded Willamette University, the first university west of the Mississippi.

Ursula K. Le Guin See page 82.

Barry Lopez (1945–) writes essays and books about the outdoors. His book *Arctic Dreams* won the National Book Award. He has lived in Oregon since 1968.

Bernard Malamud (1914–1986) was a novelist and educator who wrote *The Natural, The Assistant, The Fixer,* and *A New Life.* He was born in Brooklyn, New York, and taught at Oregon State University for many years.

Edwin Markham (1852–1940), born in Oregon City, was a poet. Many of his poems, such as "The Man with the Hoe" and "Lincoln, the Man of the People," had a political slant.

Ahmad Rashad

Tom McCall (1913–1983) served as governor of Oregon from 1967 to 1975. Born in Massachusetts, he attended high school in Oregon and later graduated from the University of Oregon with a degree in journalism. He is best known for his achievements in the environmental sector.

John McLoughlin See page 42.

Joe Meek See page 47.

Tiffeny Milbrett See page 87.

Wayne Morse See page 92.

Bethenia Owens-Adair See page 57.

Linus Carl Pauling (1901–1994), born in Portland, was a chemist who received the 1954 Nobel Prize in chemistry for his work on chemical bonding. He also received the 1963 Nobel Peace Prize for his work in opposing the testing of nuclear weapons in the atmosphere.

Linus Carl Pauling

Henry Lewis Pittock See page 113.

Steven Prefontaine (1951–1975) was a track star at the University of Oregon who set a series of world records.

Ahmad Rashad (1949–) is a sports announcer and former football player who spent 10 years as a receiver in the National Football League (NFL). An All-American running back at the University of Oregon, he was a four-time Pro Bowl selection in the NFL.

Susan Raye (1944–), born in Eugene, is a country singer known for her 1972 hit "I've Got a Happy Heart."

John Reed (1887–1920), a native of Portland, was a journalist. His book *Ten Days That Shook the World* was an eyewitness account of the 1917 communist revolution in Russia.

Mark Rothko (1903–1970) was an abstract painter born in Latvia. He moved to Portland with his family in 1913 and later settled in New York. Many of his paintings depict large blocks of color.

Julia Ruuttila (1907–1991) was a journalist and activist who supported striking logging workers and tried to help African Americans from Vanport who lost their homes in a 1948 flood. She was from Portland.

Curtis Salgado (1954–) is a blues singer and harmonica player based in Portland. He was the inspiration for the Blues Brothers characters played by John Belushi and Dan Aykroyd in the late 1970s.

Doc Severinsen (1927–), born in Arlington, is a jazz trumpeter who led the band on Johnny Carson's *Tonight Show* during the 1970s and 1980s.

Mary Decker Slaney (1958–) is a runner from Eugene. She broke many national and world records.

Mary Decker Slaney

Doc Severinsen

William Stafford (1914–1993) was a poet and teacher who sometimes wrote poems inspired by the natural beauty of the Northwest. His books of poetry include *Traveling Through the Dark* (1962), *The Earth* (1974), and *Who Are You Really, Wanderer?* (1993).

William Simon U'Ren See page 65.

Frances Fuller Victor (1826–1902) was a poet, writer, and historian who wrote the two-volume *History of Oregon.*

Henry Villard See page 56.

Lindsay Wagner (1949–) is a TV and movie actress best known for her portrayal of Jaime Sommers in the 1970s television series *The Bionic Woman*. A successful author, she has written several books on beauty and personal health. She spent part of her childhood in Portland and attended the University of Oregon.

Marie Watt (1967–) is a Native American sculptor who lives and works in Portland. Most of her work explores Native American history and contemporary life.

Opal Whiteley See page 19.

Nathaniel Jarvis Wyeth (1802–1856) was a trader and explorer who built Fort William at the mouth of the Willamette River.

RESOURCES

BOOKS

Nonfiction

Benoit, Peter. *The Louisiana Purchase*. New York: Children's Press, 2012.
Friedman, Mel. *The Oregon Trail*. New York: Children's Press, 2013.
Hopping, Lorraine Jean. *Chief Joseph: The Voice for Peace*. New York: Sterling, 2010.
King, David C. *Herbert Hoover*. Tarrytown, N.Y.: Marshall Cavendish Benchmark, 2010.
Lace, William W. *Sir Francis Drake*. New York: Chelsea House, 2009.
Meeker, Ezra. *Ox-Team Days on the Oregon Trail*. Springville, Utah: Cedar Fort, 2013.
Miller, Brandon Marie. *Women of the Frontier: 16 Tails of Trailblazing Homesteaders, Entrepreneurs, and Rabble-Rousers*. Chicago: Chicago Review Press, 2012.
Roza, Greg. *Oregon Past and Present*. New York: Rosen Central, 2010.

Fiction

Bunting, Eve. *The Summer of Riley*. New York: Joanna Cotler, 2001.
Cleary, Beverly. *The Ramona Collection*. New York: HarperTrophy, 2006.
Hermes, Patricia. *A Perfect Place*. New York: Scholastic Inc., 2002.
Thompson, Gare. *Our Journey West: The Oregon Trail Adventures of Sarah Marshall*. Washington, D.C.: National Geographic, 2003.
Van Leeuwen, Jean. *Bound for Oregon*. New York: Puffin, 1996.
Veltfort, Ruhama. *The Promised Land*. Minneapolis: Milkweed Editions, 1998.

INDEX

Page numbers in *italics* indicate illustrations.

49th parallel, *47*
116th Depot Brigade, *67*

A. C. Gilbert Discovery Village, 101
Addy, Obo, 85, *85*
Advocate newspaper, 71
African Americans, 52, 58, 63, 68, 70, 71
agriculture, 40, 42, 43–44, 45, 50, *51*, 54, 55, *64*, 68, 71, 71, 72, 75, 78, *78*, *98*, *102*, 103, *104*
Ainge, Danny, 85, 133
Albany, 111
Alien Land Act (1922), 68
Ameri, Goli, 133, *133*
The American Village (Henry Warre), *42*
animal life, 18–19, 20, *22*, 23, 31, 32, 37–38, 44, *44*, 46, *55*, 72, 103, *103*, 109, 112
Armisen, Fred, 83, *83*
art, 30, *42*, *44*, 76, 80–81, 137
artifacts, 24, *24*, *27*, *37*
Ashland, 80, 85
Astoria, *40*, 41, 58, *58*, 59, 108, 133
Astor, John Jacob, *40*, 41, *41*, 133
Auburn ghost town, 114

Backman, Walter, 133
Baker City, 114
Balch, Frederic Homer, 81–82, 133
Barlow Road, 44
Barlow, Sam, 44
Basin and Range Region, 12, 15, 16, 25, 27
Beard, James, 133
beaver (state animal), 38, 46, 96
Beaverton, *76*, *81*, *99*, *101*
Belluschi, Pietro, 80, *80*
Berry, Don, 82, 133
Bierstadt, Albert, *44*
birds, 19, *19*, 20, 27, 108, 109
"Black Laws," 71
Blanc, Mel, 83–84, 133
Blue Mountains, 12, 15, 44
Boardman, 114
Bonneville, Benjamin Louis Eulalie de, 133
Bonneville Lock and Dam, *21*, 69, 70, 73
borders, 9, 11, 15, 39, 46, 47, 61
Bottle Bill, 21, 92
Bowerman, Bill, 86, 101, 133
bracero program. *See* Mexican Farm Labor Program.
British North West Company, 37, 41
Broken Top Mountain, *12*
Brownstein, Carrie, 83, *83*

Callahan, John, 85, 133
Camp Adair, 70
Cannady, Beatrice Morrow, 71, *71*, *133*
Cannon Beach, 108
canoes, *12*, 28, 29, 30, 31, 32
Cape Blanco Lighthouse, 109
Cape Kiwanda, *13*
Carr, Mary Jane, 82
Carver, Raymond, 134
carvings, 30
Cascade Mountains, 12, *12*, 13, 14, 16, 17, 18, 55, 67, 72
Cayuse people, 27, 32, 115
cedar plank salmon, 79
Celilo Falls, 55
Chambers, Richard, 92
Chin, Marilyn, 134
Chinook people, 28, *30*, 32, 41, 134
Christianity, 43
circuit courts, 94
Civilian Conservation Corps (CCC), 69, *69*
Civil War, 52
Clark, William, 38–40, *39*, 108
Clatsop people, 28, 41, 59
Clearwater River, 39
Cleary, Beverly, 81, *81*
climate, 16, 17, 42
clothing, 28, 30, 40, 92, 114
coastline, 11, 13, *13*, 16, 19, 21, 25, 28, 31, *34*, *50*, *72*
Coast Range Region, 12, 13, 16
Columbia Gorge Discovery Center, 113
Columbia Plateau, 12, 15, 16, 24, 25, 26–27, 32
Columbia Rediviva (ship), 38
Columbia River, 7, 10, *21*, 24, 28, *29*, 41, 44, 55, 58, 69, 70, 73, 134
Columbia River Gorge, 69, 113
Columbia River Maritime Museum, 108
Colvig, Pinto, 134
commissioners, 95
computer industry, 101
Concomly (Chinook leader), 134
Constitution of the United States, 66
construction industry, 49, 70, 72, *100*, 101, 105
Cooper, Alice, 42
Coos Bay, 51, 109
Corps of Discovery, 39–40, *39*, 108
Corvallis, 70, 80
counties, 94, *95*
Court of Appeals, 94
Crater Lake, 9, 14, *14*, 73
Curry, George, 54
Curry, Ann, 134, *134*

The Dalles, 24, 43, 44, 58, 80, 113
dance, 30–31
Davis, Harold Lenoir (H. L.), 82, 134
Deschutes River, 15
"direct voting," 65, 89
diseases, 43, 45
Dixon, Roscoe Lee, 58, *58*
Douglas, David, 134
Douglas fir trees, 17, 59, 104, 134
Drake, Sir Francis, *34*, 35
Dungeness crabs, *78*, *79*
Duniway, Abigail Scott, 65, 66, *66*

Ecola State Park, *8*
education, 80, *81*, 101
elections, 64–65, 89, 94
electricity, 13, *67*, 69
elevation, 9, *10*, 11, 14, 15
elk, 18, *18*, 19, *24*, 26, 31, *97*
Elkhorn Mountain, 15
Ellsbury, Jacoby, 134, *134*
emery, 105
endangered species, 19, *19*
Engelbart, Douglas, 101, *101*
English exploration, *34*, 35
environmental protection, 20, 21, *72*, *72*
ethnic groups, *76*, *77*
Eugene, *76*, *78*, 80
European exploration, *7*, *34*, 35, *36*
Evergreen Aviation & Space Museum, 111, *111*
executive branch of government, 91, 93

First Street, *48*
fishing industry, 64, 103, 105, 109. *See also* salmon-canning.
flooding, 16, 31
foods, 24, 26, 27, 28, 31, 32, 38, 40, 45, *57–58*, *58*, *76*, *78*, *79*, *79*, *105*
Forest Grove, 80
forests, 17, 18, *18*, 19, 20, 24, 26, *59*, *59*, *72*, 104, 108
Fort Clatsop, 39, *73*, 108
Fort George, 41
Fort Nez Perce, *37*
Fort Stevens, 70
Fort Vancouver, 41
Fort William, 137
Four Rivers Cultural Center, 115
France, *7*, 38
Franklin, Jerry, 20
Frenchglen, 115
fresh pear and goat cheese salad, *79*, *79*
fur trade, 36–38, *37*, 41, 46, 133

General Electric, *56*
ghost towns, 114
Gilbert, Alfred Carlton (A. C.), 101, 134
glaciers, 15
gold, 50–51, *50*, 52, 55, 114
Gold Beach, 109
Golden Hind (ship), 34
Gold Hill, 110
governors, 54, 69, 93, *93*, 136
Grand Coulee Dam, 70
Grand Ronde Reservation, *54*
Grant Park, 81
Grants Pass, *67*
Gray, Robert, 38, 134
Great Basin, 24
Great Britain, 41, 46–47
Great Depression, 68–69, 70, 94
Green, Edith Starrett, 90, *90*
Gresham, *76*
Griffen, Henry, 114
Groening, Matt, 84–85, *84*, 135
gross state product, 100

Harris, Moses, 135
Hatfield, Mark, 93, *93*
Haycox, Ernest, 83, *83*
Haystack Rock, 108, *108*
hazelnuts, 78, *79*, 104
Hells Canyon, 9, 12, 15, *15*
Henderson, Lucy Ann, 45–46
Hewlett-Packard corporation, 101
High Desert Museum, 113
Hinmuuttu-yalatlat. *See* Joseph (Nez Perce chief).
Homowo African Arts and Cultures, 85
Hood River, 92, 114
Hoover Dam, 70
Hoover, Herbert, 94, 111
Hoover-Minthorn House Museum, 111
horses, 32–33, *33*, 44, *67*, 80, *103*
House of Representatives, 92
housing, *26*, 27, 28, 31, 70, 80
Hudson's Bay Company, 41, 46, 81
Hughes, Howard, 111
Huntley, Jodi, 135
hydroelectric power, 13, 69

Inada, Lawson Fusao, 82, 135
initiatives, 65, 89
insect life, 27
Intel corporation, 101
International Rose Test Garden, 112
internment camps, 70
interstate highways, *106*
Irwin, Steve, 135
Irwin, Terri, 135, *135*
islands, 11, 12

Japanese Americans, 70, 82, 115, 135
Jamison Square, 112
Jefferson, Thomas, 38, 39
Jerstad, Luther, 135
jobs, 20, 64, *64*, 68, 69, 70, *73*, *105*
jogging, 86
John Day River, 15
Joseph (Nez Perce chief), 61, *61*, 135
judicial branch of government, 91, 94
July, Miranda, 135

Kaiser, Henry John, 70
Kaiser Shipyards, 70
Kalapuya Nation, 43
Kesey, Ken, 82, 135, *135*
Klamath Mountains, 12, 14, *67*
Klamath people, 27
Knight, Phil, 101, 135
Krakauer, Jon, 82, *82*, 135
Ku Klux Klan, 68, *68*

Ladd Marsh Wildlife Area, 115
La Grande, 115
Lake Bonneville, 69
Lake Oswego, 111
Lakeview, 70
Lane County Rodeo Arena, *68*
Lane, Joseph, 136
language, 78
Latinos, 71, *71*, 115
latitude lines, 46
laws, 20, 21, 52, 58, 64, 65, 66, 71, 72, 80, 89, 90, 91, 92, 93
Lebanon, 20
Lee, Jason, 43, *43*, 136
legislative branch of government, 66, *88*, 89, 91, 92
Le Guin, Ursula K., 82, *82*
Lewis and Clark Campsite, 108
Lewis & Clark College, 80, 85
Lewis and Clark National Historical Park, *73*
Lewis and Clark Trail, 108
Lewis, Meriwether, 38–40, *39*, 108
literature, 76, 81–82, 83, 133, 134, 135, 136

livestock, 44, *44*, 55, 68, 72, 80, 103, *103*
local government, 94–95
logging industry. *See* timber industry.
longhouses, *26*
longitude lines, 46
Lopez, Barry, 82, 136
Louisiana Purchase, 38
Lovejoy, Asa, 46
Lower Table Rock, 110, *110*

Mahonia Hall, 93
Malamud, Bernard, 136
mammoths, 23
Manifest Destiny, 43
manufacturing, 101, 103, 105
maps
  agricultural, *102*
  counties, *95*
  European exploration, *36*
  interstate highways, *106*
  mining, *102*
  national parks, *17*
  Native Americans, *25*
  population density, *76*
  Salem, *90*
  statehood, *53*
  territory, *53*
  topographical, *10*
marine life, 19, 28, *29*, 57–58, *58*, 78, *78*, *79*, 109, 109
Markham, Edwin, 136
marmots, 18, *18*
Martin, Charles Henry, 69
McCall, Tom, 136
McLoughlin House, 113
McLoughlin, John, 42, *42*, 113
McMinnville, 80, 111
Medford, 110
Meek, Joseph Lafayette, 47, *47*
Mexican Farm Labor Program, 71, *71*
Milbrett, Tiffeny, 87, *87*
mining, 50–51, *50*, 55, 57, *102*, 103, 105
missionaries, 43, 61, 113
Missouri River, 39, 44
Monteith House, 111
Monteith, Thomas, 111
Monteith, Walter, 111
Morse, Wayne, 92, *92*
Mount Ashland, 14
Mount Hood, 9, 11, 14, 44, 45, 73, 100, 114, *114*
Mount Hood Railroad, 114, *114*
Mount Jefferson, 14
Mount Mazama, 14
Museum at Warm Springs, 114
museums, 80, 108, 110, 111, *111*, 112, 114, 115
music, 31, 76, 85, 136, 137, *137*

National American Woman Suffrage Association Convention, *66*
national parks, 14, *17*, 73, *73*
Native Americans, 7, 22, 24–25, *25*, 26–27, *26*, 28–29, *29*, 30–31, *30*, 31–32, 32–33, *33*, 37, *37*, 39, *39*, 41, 43, 46, 54–55, 59, 60–61, *60*, *61*, 80–81, 115, 134, 136
Newberg, 111
New Deal programs, 69, *69*
Newport, 109
newspapers, 52, 55, 56, 71, 113
Nez Perce people, *26*, 27, 32, *33*, 60–61, *60*, *61*
Nez Perce War, *60*, 61
Nike, Inc., 101, 133, 135
North American Plate, 11, 12
Northern Pacific Railway, 56
Northern Paiute people, 27, 115
northern spotted owls, 19, *19*, 20

Olympic Games, *86*, 87, *87*
Ontario, 115
Oregon Beavers (currency), 50
Oregon City, 16, 42, *57*, 113
Oregon Coast Aquarium, 109
Oregon grapes (state flower), 18
Oregon Historical Society, 112
Oregon House of Mystery, 110
Oregonian newspaper, 113
Oregon Museum of Science and Industry, 112, *112*
Oregon Sports Hall of Fame and Museum, 85
Oregon State University, 80
Oregon Steam Navigation Company, 55
"Oregon System," 65
Oregon Territory, 47, *53*, 136
Oregon Trail, 44–46, *57*, 133
Oregon Vortex, 110
Oregon Zoo, 111
Ouragon River, 7
Overton, William, 46
Owens-Adair, Bethenia, *57*, *57*

Pacific Fur Company, *40*, 41, 42, 133
Pacific Northwest, 46
Pacific University, 80
Paiute people, *27*
Pauling, Linus Carl, 136, *136*
pemmican (dried salmon), 24, 40
Pendleton, 16, 115
Pettygrove, Francis, 46
pine trees, 59
Pittock, Henry Lewis, 113, *113*
Pittock Mansion, 113
plant life, 17–18, 19, 20, 30, 104, *104*
plates, 11–12
Platte River, 44
Polk, James K., 46, *47*
ponderosa pine trees, 18
population, 75, 76, *76*, *77*
populism, 65
Portland, 16, 42, 46, *48*, 49, *57*, 58, 62, 63, 64, 66, 67, 70, *74*, 75, 76, 80, 81, 83, 85, 94–95, 99, 100, 111–113
Portland Art Association, 80
Portland Art Museum, 80
Portland Center for the Visual Arts, 80
Portland Community College, 80–81
Portlandia (TV series), 83, *83*
Portland State University, 80
Portland Trail Blazers basketball team, 85, 133
Port Orford, 109
Prefontaine, Steven, 86–87, *86*, 136
prehistoric people, 22, 24–25
Price, Clayton "C. S.," 80
Prineville, 16

railroads, 55–57, *56*, 59, *59*, 64, 114
ranching, 60, 64, 75
Rashad, Ahmad, 136, *136*
Raye, Susan, 136
recipe, 79
recycling, 21
Reed College, 80
Reed, John, 137
referendums, 65, 89
religion, 31–32, 43

reservations, 54–55, 60, 61, 114
roadways, 70, *106*
Rogue River, 54, 110
Rogue River Wars, 54
Roosevelt, Franklin D., 69, 70
Roscoe's Oyster House, 58
Rothko, Mark, 137
Ruuttila, Julia, 137

Sacagawea (Shoshone explorer), 39, *39*, 42
sagebrush, 18, 24, 55
SAGE Center, 114
Salem, 45–46, 52, *57*, 76, 80, *90*, 94, 101
Salgado, Curtis, 137
salmon, 19, 21, *21*, 24, 26, 28, *29*, 32, 57–58, *58*, 63, 78, *79*
salmon-canning, 57–58, *58*, 63. *See also* fishing industry.
Scott, Dred, 52
sculpture, 80–81, 137
seafood chowder, 79
sea otters, 19, 37–38, 109
Seaside, 108
secretary of state, 93
segregation, 70
Senate, *88*, 92
Seneca, 16
Sermon Rock, 113
service industries, 100–101, *100*
settlers, 42, 43–46, *44*, *47*, 54
Severinsen, Doc, 137, *137*
Shakespeare festival, 85
shipbuilding industry, 70
shipping industry, 67
Shore Acres State Park, 109
shoreline. *See* coastline.
Siletz Reservation, 54
Siskiyou Mountains, 14, 110
Slaney, Mary Decker, 87, *87*, 137, *137*
slavery, 29, 31, 52
Smith, Silas B., 59
Snake River, 11, 15, *15*, 39, 44, *57*
Sorosis Park, 113
Southern Oregon State College, 80
Spanish exploration, 7, 35
Sparks Lake, *12*
sports, *12*, 85–87, *86*, *87*, 112, 133, 134, *134*, 135, 136, *136*, 137, *137*
Springfield, 110
Spruce Goose aircraft, 111, *111*
Stafford, William, 137
Stanley, John Mix, 42
state animal, 96
state bird, 19
state capital, 52, *90*
state capitol, 90, *90*, 91
state constitution, 64–65, 89
state flag, 96, *96*
state flower, 18
statehood, 52, *53*, 97
state name, 7
State of the State address, 93
state seal, 97, *97*
state shape, 10–11
steamboats, *54*, 55
Steens Mountain, 15, 115, *115*
storytelling, 31
suffrage movement, 65–66, *66*
Supreme Court, 94
Sweetwater River, 44

taboos, 31–32
Tamástslikt Cultural Institute, 115, *115*
temperance movement, 65
theater, 85
Three Sisters, 14
Tillamook, 16, 108
Tillamook Burn, 108
Tillamook Cheese Visitor's Center, 108
Tillamook Forest Center, 108
Tillamook people, 28
timber industry, 20, 54, 59, *59*, 64, 72–73, 101, 104
topographical map, *10*
tourism, 73
transcontinental railroad, 56
transportation, 28, *54*, 55–57, *56*, 67
Treasure Valley, 115
trees, 17, 18, 26, 72, 112
tulips, 104, *104*

Umatilla people, 27, 32, 115
Umpqua River, 54
Union Pacific Railroad Company, 56–57, *56*
University of Oregon, 80, 86, 101, 133, 136, 137
University of Portland, 80
University of Washington, 20
Upper Table Rock, 110
U'Ren, William Simon, 65, *65*

Vanport community, 70
Very Berry Cobbler recipe, 79
Victor, Frances Fuller, 137
Vietnam War, 92
Villard, Henry, 56, *56*
volcanoes, 12, 14
voting rights, 64–65

Wagner, Lindsay, 137
Watkuweis (Nez Perce villager), 33
Walla Walla people, 115
Wallowa Mountains, 15
Wallowa Valley, 60, 61
Warm Springs, 114
Warm Springs Indian Reservation, 114
Warre, Henry, 42, *42*
Wasco people, 28
Washington Park, 42, 112, *112*
Watt, Marie, 80–81, 137
Wentz, Harry, 80
western meadowlark (state bird), 19
Whiteley, Opal, 19, *19*
wildfires, 108
wildflowers, 18
wildlife. *See* animal life; insect life; marine life; plant life.
Willamalane Park and Recreation District, 110, *110*
Willamette Lowland, 12, 13
Willamette River, 13, 41, 55
Willamette Shore Trolley, 111
Willamette University, 80, 136
Willamette Valley, 16, 40, 42, 44, 45, 46, 52, 54, 55, 103–104
windstorms, 16
Works Progress Administration, 69
World War I, 67–68, *67*, 94
World War II , 69, 70, 72
Wyeth, Nathaniel Jarvis, 137

Yaquina Head Lighthouse, 109, *109*

AUTHOR'S TIPS AND SOURCE NOTES

Several books on Oregon proved valuable in my research for this book. Among them are *Oregon's Promise: An Interpretive History*, by David Peterson del Mar; *The Great Northwest: A History*, by Oscar Osburn Winther; *Landscapes of Promise: The Oregon Story, 1800–1940*, by William G. Robbins; and *The Oregon Indians: Voices from Two Centuries*, edited by Stephen Dow Beckham. I find it is most useful to read full-length histories, taking extensive notes, and then to explore Web sites to gather current information.

Photographs ©: age fotostock/new leaf: cover; akg-Images, London/Waldemar Abegg: 54; Alamy Images: 108 (Buddy Mays), 100 (D. Hurst), 99 right, 103 (Danita Delimont), 89 right, 90 right (Dennis MacDonald), 83 bottom (Everett Collection Historical), 136 left (Everett Collection Inc.), 110 bottom (Kevin Schafer), 8, 9 (Peter Haigh), 12 (Reimar), 73 (Ron Niebrugge), 115 bottom (WorldFoto); AP Images: 88, 89 (Don Ryan), 134 top (Elise Amendola), 137 bottom (George Clark/Hattiesburg American), 133 top (Lawrence Jackson), 81; Art Resource, NY: 23 top right, 30 (George Catlin/Smithsonian American Art Museum, Washington, DC), 42 top (Henry James Warre/The New York Public Library); Bridgeman Art Library International Ltd., London/New York: 44 (Albert Bierstadt/Butler Institute of American Art, Youngstown, OH/Gift of Joseph G. Butler III), 22 top, 23 top left (David Nockels/Private Collection/Look and Learn), 29 (Ernest Berke/Private Collection/Peter Newark Pictures), 35 top right, 39, 23 bottom, 33, 122 (Private Collection/Peter Newark American Pictures), 4 top center, 22 bottom, 32 (Private Collection/The Stapleton Collection), 48 top, 49 top left (Royal Geographical Society, London, UK); Corbis Images: 5 top left, 51, 56 top, 66 bottom, 69 (Bettmann), 81 bottom (Christina Koci Hernandez/San Francisco Chronicle), 75 right, 84 (Douglas Kirkland), 134 bottom (Gregory Pace), 82 bottom (Jurgen Frank), 59 (Michael Maslan Historic Photographs), 14 (Phil Schermeister), 104 (Ric Ergenbright), 136 right (Roger Ressmeyer), 15 (Steve Terrill), 79 top; Digital Railroad: 5 bottom, 109 bottom (Alan Majchrowicz), 9 right, 13 (Craig Tuttle), 111 (Greg Vaughn), 112 top (Janis Miglavs/Danita Delimont); DK Images/Mike Dunning: 49 bottom; Everett Collection/IFC: 83 top; Getty Images: 74, 75 (Anthony Pidgeon), 48 bottom left (C Squared Studios), 86 (Co Rentmeester), 87 right (Donald Miralle), cover inset (Emily Riddell), 92 (George Skadding), 63 bottom (Hulton Archive), 82 top (Michael Buckner), 42 bottom (MPI/Hulton Archive), 80 (Nancy R. Schiff), 135 bottom (Scott Wintrow), 94 (Stock Montage), 93 (Terry Ashe), 21 (Tim Matsui); Gibson Stock Photography: 78 top, 109 top, 121; Homowo African Arts and Cultures/Julie Keefe: 85; Inmagine: 4 bottom right, 96, 127; iStockphoto: 130 top (David Freund), 116 bottom, 130 bottom (Geoffrey Black), 48 bottom right, 123 bottom (Hannamaria Photography), 128 (Vladislav Lebedinski); Library of Congress/Harris & Ewing: 90 left; Mary Evans Picture Library: 56 bottom; Media Bakery/Daniel Hurst: 98, 99 left; Minden Pictures/Thomas Mangelsen: 4 top left, 19 top, 120; Montana Historical Society, Helena/Jos Bucktel: 47 top; Mt. Hood Railroad, Hood River, OR: 114; Nativestock.com/Marilyn "Angel" Wynn: 26, 60, 124; Newscom: 87 left, 137 top (Julian H. Gonzalez/Detroit Free Press), 101 (Richard Wisdom/San Jose Mercury News), 135 top; North Wind Picture Archives: 35 bottom, 45 (Nancy Carter), 47 bottom; Oregon Historical Society: 34 bottom, 123 top (CN 004737), 62 bottom (College Equal Suffrage Handbill/Mss 1534), 72 (Herb Alden/Oregon Journal/OrHi 91802), 37 top (Joseph Drayton/OrHi 964), 58 right (Keystone View Company/OrHi 28194), 24 (OHS Mus 4937/84), 27 (OHS Mus 72-126.9), 4 top right, 37 bottom (OHS Mus 98-1.209), 71 top, 133 bottom (Oregon Journal Collection/CN 011493), 62 top, 63 top left (OrHi 13134), 58 left (OrHi 38663), 5 top right, 67 (OrHi 38812), 57 (OrHi 4062), 65 (OrHi 49958), 68 (OrHi 54400), 66 top (OrHi 59438), 43 (OrHi 634), 71 bottom (OrHi 73286), 63 top right, 64 (Will Raymond/OrHi 6337), 50 (William V. Vells/OrHi 23436), 38; Courtesy of Oregon Museum of Science and Industry: 112 bottom; Peter Arnold Inc./M. Hamblin: 18 bottom, Pittock Mansion Collection: 113; Redux Pictures/Mark Peterson: 118; Ric Ergenbright: 115 top; ShutterStock, Inc.: 79 bottom (HD Connelly), 4 bottom left, 78 bottom (Morgan Lane Photography), 49 top right (Robert Ottokar Lindneux); Superstock, Inc.: 61 (Robert Ottokar Lindneux), back cover (Stock Connection); The Art Archive/Picture Desk/Cornelis de Vries: 34 top, 35 top left; The Granger Collection, New York: 40, 41; University of Oregon Library System/Archives and Special Collections: 19 bottom; US Mint: 116 top, 119; Vector-Images.com: 97, 126; Visuals Unlimited/Ken Lucas: 18 top; Willamalane Park & Recreation District/John Bauguess: 110 top.

Maps by Map Hero, Inc.